FAUSTINA,
SAINT *for* OUR TIMES

A Personal Look at Her Life,
Spirituality, and Legacy

FAUSTINA,
SAINT *for* OUR TIMES

A Personal Look at Her Life,
Spirituality, and Legacy

Rev. George W. Kosicki, CSB
with David C. Came

MARIAN PRESS
STOCKBRIDGE MA 01263
PRO CHRISTO ET ECCLESIA

2011

Available from:
Marian Helpers Center
Stockbridge, MA 01263

Prayerline: 1-800-804-3823
Orderline: 1-800-462-7426
Website: www.marian.org

Imprimi Potest:
Very Rev. Daniel Cambra, MIC
Provincial Superior
The Blessed Virgin Mary, Mother of Mercy Province
April 2, 2010

Library of Congress Catalog Number: 2010926013
ISBN: 978-1-59614-226-8

Cover Art: Painting of St. Faustina based on her passport photo
copyright © Marian Fathers of the Immaculate Conception of the B.V.M.
Design of Cover and Pages: Kathy Szpak

Editing and Proofreading: David Came, Mary Flannery,
Dan Valenti, and Andrew Leeco

For texts from the English Edition of
Diary of St. Maria Faustina Kowalska

Nihil Obstat:
George H. Pearce, SM
Former Archbishop of Suva, Fiji

Imprimatur:
Joseph F. Maguire
Bishop of Springfield, MA
April 9, 1984

Printed in the United States of America

DEDICATION

*Blessed John Paul II, Pope Benedict XVI,
and the devotees of The Divine Mercy
throughout the world*

CONTENTS

ACKNOWLEDGMENTS 9

FOREWORD 11

PREFACE 15

INTRODUCTION 19

CHAPTER 1: THE LIFE OF ST. FAUSTINA 25
    From Farm to Convent: 1905-30 27
    Devotions of Divine Mercy: 1930-38 33

CHAPTER 2: THE MISSION OF ST. FAUSTINA 45
    Revelations 47
    Motto of St. Faustina: 'God and Souls' 52
    The Holy Eucharist, the Presence of Mercy 55
    Reconciliation: Tribunal of Mercy 60
    Living Out Her Mission of Mercy 64

CHAPTER 3: THE SPIRITUAL LIFE OF ST. FAUSTINA 69
    Basic Spirituality 71
    The Unique Features of the Spirituality of St. Faustina . . 73
    The Gospel Elements of Her Spiritual Life 78

CHAPTER 4: FAUSTINA: A BLENDING OF EAST AND WEST . . . 83
    The 'Spark' from Poland: Where East and West Meet . . 85
    Treasures of the Christian East in the Life of St. Faustina . . 89
    Other Elements of Eastern Spirituality Stressed
       by John Paul II in *Orientale Lumen* 93
    The Treasures of Western Christianity in the Life
       of St. Faustina 99

CHAPTER 5: FAUSTINA: SAINT FOR THE THIRD MILLENNIUM . . 103
    Spread of The Divine Mercy Message and Devotion . . . 105
    St. Faustina and Pope John Paul II 106
    Faustina's Continuing Mission of Mercy 119

CHAPTER 6: OUR RESPONSE 125

It's All about Trust 127

A Life of Prayer 132

How Do We Show Mercy? 133

Our Response to the Challenges of St. Faustina,
Blessed John Paul II, and Pope Benedict XVI 137

DIVINE MERCY PRAYERS 143

CHRONOLOGY OF DIVINE MERCY 155

ACKNOWLEDGMENTS

A special thanks to David Came, my coauthor and the executive editor of Marian Press, for the generous gift of himself in expanding, revising, and editing *Faustina, Saint for Our Times*. His expertise focused the text more clearly on St. Faustina, especially in the final chapters "Faustina: Saint for the Third Millennium" and "Our Response." I particularly appreciate his expanding St. Faustina's continuing mission of mercy to include the papacy of Benedict XVI and the World Apostolic Congresses on Mercy. With new material, he also highlighted more St. Faustina's prophetic role. Finally, he developed further many of the entries in the "Chronology of Divine Mercy," which is provided at the end of the book.

Thanks also to Mary Flannery, former associate editor of Marian Press, who, along with David Came, encouraged me to revise and expand this book: to Dan Valenti, senior editor of Marian Press, for his review of the manuscript and editing; to Andrew Leeco, the associate editor of Marian Press, for his proofreading; to Kathy Szpak, a designer at the Marian Helpers Center who designed the cover and the pages; to Gina Shultis, marketing manager of Marian Press, for her marketing plans for the book; and to Pat Menatti who typed this expansion and personalization of the text.

FOREWORD

It is obvious that Divine Providence was preparing my dear friend, Fr. George Kosicki, CSB, to write on St. Faustina and the whole Divine Mercy devotion when his mother was asked by some Marian priests to paint The Divine Mercy image only a few years after the saint's death. This book represents one of the most fascinating of Fr. George's many efforts to spread devotion to The Divine Mercy. Even those familiar with the history and meaning of this devotion will learn much from *Faustina, Saint for Our Times.* Father George develops a number of new areas of interest like the relationship of Eastern spirituality to the experience and insights of St. Faustina. He also explains the painful misunderstanding and disapproval of this devotion early on, as well as the gradual changes in attitude motivated largely by the Archbishop of Krakow who became Blessed John Paul II.

Best of all are Fr. George's own discussions of the spiritual teachings contained in the *Diary* and life of St. Faustina. The various Christian schools and movements of spirituality do not differ essentially from each other since all are based on the Gospels themselves. All these approaches to the spiritual journey are examined and guided by Tradition and the Church. However, there are different emphases in each or at least different ways of expressing key ideas. It is these differences that enrich the vast library of Catholic spiritual literature. This book focuses on the special emphasis of The Divine Mercy devotion, especially the meaning and depth of God's mercy and the necessary complete trust and confidence that this mercy summons forth from the human heart and soul.

Anyone familiar with the history of mysticism will have to smile at the familiar pattern of God's preferences — He exalts the lowly *again*. Saint Faustina, with her two winters of education and her trying spiritual preparation, as well as her premature, difficult death, brings to mind a whole line of simple, devout, intensely dedicated, and humble young women whom God has chosen to be prophetesses in His Church. Beginning with martyrs like Agnes, Catherine, and Lucy, the history of the Church has a remarkable line of young women to whom were revealed the mysteries of the kingdom of God. One thinks immediately of Joan of Arc, who brought an end to the Hundred Years' War and saved her homeland for the Catholic faith by being docile to the heavenly voices. Then there is the great Catherine of Siena, whose visions historically saved the papacy. There is a whole line of visionary women who have shaped Catholic devotion in modern times: Margaret Mary, Bernadette, Catherine Labouré, and the children of Fatima — all of these are "the little ones" whom Jesus has spoken to. Although not a vision- ary in the sense of the others, one cannot fail to mention how the Holy Spirit has affected the history of the Church by that other young woman who died so painfully, Thérèse of Lisieux.

Parenthetically, it is worthwhile to remember that the teachings of the Church on private revelations, even those given to canonized saints, indicate that they do not have the authority or inerrancy of Sacred Scripture. Private revelations always reflect the personal experience of the individual who has received these special graces. Their visions and messages are colored by their knowledge and their own personal thoughts and understanding of the visions they received. It is important to keep in mind that any of these revelations given by the Holy Spirit to the Church at a particular time are really encounters of the finite with the Infinite. Visionaries are apparently chosen because they will be docile and honest, and will avoid controversy. They cannot, however, avoid including their own ideas in the description of what they experience, even when they do their very best to be objective. Only a visionary like St. Bernadette, who received a very simple and brief message, can keep his or her ideas to a bare minimum.

Probably many of the visions of St. Faustina fall into the category that St. John of the Cross calls intellectual visions. In this case, the mind of the individual under the inspiration of grace seeks adequate forms and words to express the truths he or she experiences. It's obvious, for example, that any vision of the Holy Trinity must be like this because no human can perceive the infinity of God. One can perceive this personal quality of intellectual visions in St. Faustina's fascinating description of her Trinitarian experience. I have tried to explore some of these profound and mysterious concepts in my book *A Still Small Voice* — a review of the Church's teaching on private revelation (Ignatius Press). When we understand as much as we can about this profoundly mysterious topic of private revelations and visions, we are far better prepared to learn from them. We can avoid a kind of fundamentalism and excessive literalism that can cause trouble even with the interpretation of the Holy Scripture, which is public revelation.

The spiritual doctrine and meaning of Divine Mercy, which is communicated so effectively to the pure and suffering soul of St. Faustina, is well summed up by Fr. George. Of course, he is guided in this by *Rich in Mercy* (*Dives in Misericordia*), the magnificent encyclical on Divine Mercy by Blessed John Paul II. The *Diary of St. Faustina* can be an awesome document to approach because of its length, complexity, and mysterious origins as private revelations. In this book, the content and meaning of the *Diary* are very effectively analyzed and related to the present situation in the Church as well as to world history.

This is a book to keep for a long time. You may want to have your own personal copy so that you can write marginal notes and underline. You will also want to share copies with friends who are sincerely seeking to grow in the love of God and Christian discipleship. It can also be shared with Christians of other denominations, especially Eastern Orthodox friends. This book may be the source of a special grace to the large number of people returning to the Church now who are troubled by the memory of the years when they were off the track. The mystery of Divine Mercy is an essential and most powerful element in the Christian life. Here you will find it very well explored through the life and experiences of the great and humble mystic of our times.

Fr. Benedict J. Groeschel, CFR

PREFACE

Helena Kowalska was born in the little rural village of Glogowiec, Poland, in the year 1905. As early as the age of seven, she heard the voice of the Lord in her soul, calling her to a more perfect way of life. As a result, just before her 20th birthday with hardly a penny to her name and without her parents' permission, she journeyed alone by rail to Warsaw to pursue a call to the religious life. A year later, she entered the convent of the Sisters of Our Lady of Mercy.

Over the next few years, Sr. Maria Faustina of the Most Blessed Sacrament (Helena's chosen religious name) deepened her life of prayer and grew strong in her practice of the Christian virtues. She regularly performed the most menial tasks for her community: as cook, gardener, and porter, for example. But she was noted especially for her cheerfulness, for her care for the poor who came to the convent seeking food, and for her loving kindness to the girls whom the sisters trained and educated in their houses. In fact, many of the sisters knew of her desire for holiness, and so they trusted her and came to her for counsel and advice — so much so that she earned the nickname "the dump," because they were always "dumping" their problems on her.

After an intense period of spiritual purification that occurred early in her life as a religious, our Lord brought her into a special intimacy with His merciful Heart. She began to receive mystical revelations, visions, locutions, and prophecies, all focused on the same theme: the mercy of the Lord for the lost and the broken. At the command of her spiritual director, she recorded her spiritual experiences in her *Diary*, which is now regarded as an outstanding spiritual classic of the

20th century and a miracle in itself, given that Sr. Faustina had barely two winters of elementary education!

Sister Faustina also bore many sufferings: from the tuberculosis which gradually ravaged her body, to the uncharitable misinterpretation of her growing physical weakness by many of her fellow sisters, to her anguish about her own seeming inability to carry out the Lord's requests to her. He had asked her to initiate several forms of devotion to His Divine Mercy throughout the world, that a wayward and wounded mankind — already headed for a second world war — might soon learn to ask for His mercy, completely trust in His mercy, and be merciful to others, as He is merciful.

Sister Faustina offered up all her prayers, works, and sufferings, in union with the crucified Jesus, for mercy upon poor sinners, especially those who have lost their trust in God's goodness. In addition, our Lord frequently appeared to her as a child, asking her to learn from Him the lesson of spiritual childhood: to approach God with humility and trust, as a little child would do. These themes of her spiritual life echo the "little way" of another great mystic of modern times, St. Thérèse of Lisieux.

Sister Faustina died on October 5, 1938, but her mission was far from over. In fact, it was only just beginning. She wrote: "I feel certain that my mission will not come to an end upon my death, but will begin. O doubting souls, I will draw aside the veils of heaven to convince you of God's goodness" (*Diary*, 281). By her heavenly intercessions, St. Faustina has been fulfilling that promise ever since, obtaining countless graces and miracles for suffering souls from the compassionate Heart of Jesus:

> O my Jesus, each of Your saints reflects one of Your virtues; I desire to reflect Your compassionate Heart, full of mercy; I want to glorify it. Let Your mercy, O Jesus, be impressed upon my heart and soul like a seal, and this will be my badge in this and the future life. Glorifying Your mercy is the exclusive task of my life (*Diary*, 1242).

Perhaps the message and mission of St. Faustina to the modern world was best summed up by the Holy Father, Pope John Paul II, in his homily for her beatification on Divine Mercy Sunday, April 18, 1993:

> Her mission continues and is yielding astonishing fruit. It is truly marvelous how her devotion to the merciful Jesus is spreading in our contemporary world and gaining so many human hearts! This is doubtlessly a sign of the times — a sign of our twentieth century. The balance of this century which is now ending … presents a deep restlessness and fear of the future. Where, if not in the Divine Mercy, can the world find refuge and the light of hope? Believers understand that perfectly.

Rev. Seraphim Michalenko, MIC
Director of the Association of Marian Helpers
Vice-Postulator Emeritus of
the Cause for the Canonization of St. Faustina,
Director Emeritus of
the John Paul II Institute of Divine Mercy

INTRODUCTION

I want to tell you about my favorite saint, who is important not only to me but to the Church of the third millennium. In religious life, she is called Sr. Faustina. Her full religious name is Sr. Maria Faustina of the Most Blessed Sacrament.

I first came to know of her in the early 1940s, when Marian priests living in my home parish of St. Teresa of Avila in Detroit, Michigan, asked my mother to paint an image of Sr. Faustina's vision of the merciful Jesus. However, my mother's specialty was not portrait painting, and her attempt was not satisfactory. Nevertheless, in 1946, when I entered my religious community, she gave me a framed print of the merciful Jesus done in Mexico, modeled after a prayer card from the mid-1930s of the original Divine Mercy image under the direction of St. Faustina with the words *Jezu ufam Tobie!* ("Jesus, I trust in You" in Polish). It has hung above my bed for over a half century.

It wasn't until 1985, during an extended hermitage retreat, that I felt called to proclaim God's mercy full-time, according to the revelations of Sr. Faustina. This I have done through continued prayer, studying, writing, teaching, and preaching.

I have immersed myself in the *Diary of St. Faustina*. I have read it repeatedly, both in its original Polish and in English over the years. This was the beginning of my deepening personal knowledge and growing relationship with St. Faustina. This daily reading of her *Diary* led me to develop the *Thematic Concordance to the Diary of St. Maria Faustina Kowalska* (Marian Press). It was an expression of my training in the scientific field of biochemistry by which I summarized the content of each paragraph in the *Diary*. *The Thematic Concordance* grew into an extensive topical index that covers more than 90 major themes and 7,000 sub-themes in the *Diary* — many with multiple cross references. This work plunged me even more deeply into the ocean of mercy and the life of St. Faustina. It has become, some would say, *the* major work that has led to hundreds of articles and more than 40 books, mostly on The Divine Mercy message and devotion. This work on the *Thematic Concordance* also encouraged me to teach at conferences and group presentations, which also led to multiple presentations on TV and radio.

I used the *Thematic Concordance* to prepare: *Revelations of Divine Mercy: Daily Readings from the Diary of St. Faustina Kowalska* (Servant Books/St. Anthony Messenger Press), a month at a time on one topic; *Mercy Minutes: Daily Gems of St. Faustina to Transform Your Prayer Life* (Marian Press); *Mercy Minutes with Jesus: Praying Daily on the Words of Jesus from the Diary of St. Faustina,* (Marian Press) with prayer responses to Jesus; and *John Paul II: The Great Mercy Pope* (Marian Press).

In addition, my five pilgrimages to Poland and to Vilnius, Lithuania, fostered and deepened my relationship with St. Faustina. The pilgrimages, organized by Sr. Isabel Bettwy, deepened my understanding and appreciation of Sr. Faustina as we visited the significant places in her life:

- ❖ Renewing my own Baptism with Holy Water from the font in which St. Faustina was baptized in Swinice, Poland.

- ❖ Praying in the simple, one-room cottage in Swinice, Poland, where she was born and grew up.

- ❖ Prostrating myself in the Cathedral of St. Stanislaus Kostka in Lódz, Poland, where Faustina prostrated and surrendered her life to the Lord.

- ❖ Visiting Plock, where Jesus appeared to her and asked that she paint an image of the apparition of the radiating merciful Jesus (see *Diary*, 47). There, we celebrated the Sacrament of Reconciliation and made a Holy Hour of Adoration in preparation for a glorious celebration of Mass. It was a high point of our pilgrimage.

❖ In Vilnius, we prayed the Chaplet of Divine Mercy (see *Diary*, 474-76) where St. Faustina was taught to pray the chaplet.

❖ In Warsaw, we celebrated Mass at the restored convent, which is the Mother House of the Sisters of Our Lady of Mercy.

❖ In Krakow/Lagiewniki, we celebrated Mass at the main altar of the chapel where St. Faustina made her novitiate and where she died and was buried.

All this prayer, study, publishing of books, pilgrimages, and teachings led me to a full-time commitment to promoting The Divine Mercy message and devotion, with St. Faustina as my sister and the "great apostle of Divine Mercy in our time" (John Paul II, Mercy Sunday, 1994).

So it comes as no surprise that in the fall of 1992, while at the Shrine of Sr. Faustina in Lagiewniki (a suburb of Krakow) as chaplain for a Divine Mercy pilgrimage to Poland, I came to know her in a more personal way. Our tour bus was ready to depart, but two pilgrims were missing. I anxiously went back into the shrine to look for them. As I passed by the tomb of Sr. Faustina, I heard in my heart: "I am your sister, trust even more!" These words stayed with me for the rest of the pilgrimage and for weeks afterward. I hand printed them on three-by-five index cards and put them at the door of my house, at the entrance to the chapel, and on the bathroom mirror: TRUST in JESUS EVEN MORE! These words of trust have now become a "screensaver" for many computers.

To trust in Jesus is the heart of the life and spirituality of St. Faustina. In this book, *Faustina, Saint for Our Times*, I will introduce you to her life and spirituality — which I call "The Merciful Way." The early chapters will focus on her life, mission, and spirituality. I will also tell you about Blessed John Paul II's personal involvement in spreading The Divine Mercy message and devotion.

I cover how St. Faustina and her spirituality blend traditions of the East and the West in Chapter 4, including a discussion of icons and The Divine Mercy image. In Chapter 5, you will learn why Faustina is the saint of the third millennium and how her mission continues in the present day. This chapter provides fascinating highlights of St. Faustina's influence on Pope John Paul II and now Pope Benedict XVI. We even see how certain prophecies of hers have been fulfilled in our time.

Then, in Chapter 6, we will consider our response to The Divine Mercy message and St. Faustina — from trusting in the Lord to practical tips on living mercifully. Further, I've included some of Fastina's prayers and excerpts from her *Diary* at the end of the book, especially inspiring ones for daily use or for special occasions of need. At the very end is a chronology of Divine Mercy to help you keep in mind the broader historical perspective on St. Faustina's life, her beatification and canonization, and her continuing mission of mercy in our time.

So, why read this book?

The Divine Mercy message and devotion is an urgent message for the whole world to hear and act upon. Pope John Paul II cried out to the world at the beatification of Sr. Faustina: "Where, if not in the Divine Mercy, can the world find refuge and the light of hope?" Then, at the Shrine of The Divine Mercy in Poland, when he entrusted the world to Divine Mercy, he proclaimed: "There is nothing that mankind needs more than Divine Mercy."

This is the essence of St. Faustina's mission of mercy. It reminds me of how Mary Flannery, a former associate editor of Marian Press, pointed out that this book on St. Faustina is more than just a biography — it is a deeper, personal look into her life and spirituality and her continuing mission of spreading the message of Divine Mercy. It is an urgent mission to both the Church and to the whole world so desperately in need of mercy! Now is the time for mercy.

Pope John Paul II frequently repeated the words our Lord spoke to St. Faustina about this urgency, Among them are these powerful words, **Mankind will not have peace until it turns with trust to My mercy** (*Diary*, 300).

Note to the Reader: Following the conventions of the *Diary*, throughout the text in this book, the words of Jesus are in bold and the words of Mary are italicized.

It is my prayer that this book will help you get to know St. Faustina, who is "the great apostle of Divine Mercy in our time," as John Paul II put it. May it also help you become a witness to that mercy, as you join St. Faustina in her mission of mercy in our day. Consider these words of encouragement from Faustina about how her mission continues with new possibilities after her death:

> O my Jesus, I now embrace the whole world and ask You for mercy for it. ... And when I stand at the foot of Your throne, the first hymn that I will sing will be one to Your mercy. Poor earth, I will not forget you. Although I feel that I will be immediately drowned in God as in an ocean of happiness, that will not be an obstacle to my returning to earth to encourage souls and incite them to trust in God's mercy. Indeed, this immersion in God will give me the possibility of boundless action (*Diary*, 1582).

CHAPTER 1

❖❖❖❖❖❖

The Life of
St. Faustina

FROM FARM TO CONVENT: 1905-30

BORN IN THE HEART OF POLAND

Faustina was born in the small village of Glogowiec, Poland, near Lodz, on August 25, 1905. Two days later, Stanislaus Kowalski and his wife, Marianna, took their third child to nearby Swinice, where she was baptized "Helena" in the parish church of St. Casimir. One of 10 children of a poor farmer and carpenter, she knew what it was to live simply in a small cottage, doing chores around the house and working on the farm. She and her sisters took turns attending Mass on Sundays, sharing the one good dress they owned.

Religion was central to the Kowalski family. Stanislaus sang out his daily prayers early in the morning before work. While his daughter was young, he taught her short prayers and how to read the lives of saints and missionaries, Helen, as she was called by her family, was a gifted storyteller. She fascinated other children by repeating the stories to them. Her mother's tender compassion and dedication to her husband and family also influenced the young girl.

Unusually drawn to spiritual pursuits, Helen was seven when she first heard a voice in her soul challenging her to a more perfect way of life (see *Diary*, 7). At the age of nine, she received her First Holy Communion.

Since Polish schools had been closed during the Russian occupation, Helen did not begin her primary education until age 12. Her schooling was cut off after two winters when officials decided to make room for younger students.

In the spring of 1921, in order to assist her parents, she went to work as a housemaid and baby-sitter in the town of Alexandrow. Her joyful spirit and natural gift of storytelling, combined with an innate skill in nurturing children, made her a favorite. Helen, however, was still drawn to a more spiritual life. After a year, she returned home and informed her parents that she wanted to join a convent. Neither paid attention to her pleas.

In the fall of 1922, Helen left home again, this time to work in Lodz. Her prayer life deepened, and she disciplined herself by fasting. The families she worked for were delighted with her goodness, helpfulness, and joyous laughter.

THE TURNING POINT

In July of 1924, she and her sister Josephine attended a dance in the park behind the Cathedral of St. Stanislaus in Lodz. There, she suddenly saw Jesus at her side. He was racked with pain, stripped of His clothing, and covered with wounds. He spoke to her: **How long shall I put up with you, and how long will you keep putting Me off?** (*Diary*, 9).

This was the turning point in her life. She ran to the cathedral, threw herself on the floor before the altar, and begged the Lord to be good enough to let her know what she should do next (see *Diary*, 9). Then she heard these words: **Go at once to Warsaw; you will enter a convent there** (*Diary*, 10).

Helen went home and packed her things. When morning came, she said good-bye to her sister and uncle, who then took her to the train for Warsaw. Obedient to the word she had heard, and with only the clothes on her back, Helen set off for the city.

In Warsaw, she knew no one. After morning Mass, a priest directed her to a woman who would help with a place to stay. Helen began her search for a convent to enter, but none would accept her until she knocked at the door of the Sisters of Our Lady of Mercy. The Mother Superior took a liking to Helen and told her to go to the Lord of the house and ask whether He would accept her. With joy, she went to the chapel and asked the Lord Jesus, "Do you accept me?" She immediately heard: **I do accept you; you are in My Heart.** On returning to Mother Superior, who asked, "Well, has the Lord accepted you?" Helen answered, "Yes." "If the

Lord has accepted," Mother responded, "then I also will accept" (*Diary*, 14).

Because Helen had no money for a sister's wardrobe, Mother suggested she continue working and set aside the needed funds. Helen regularly delivered her earnings to the convent. Within a year, she had enough. Helen Kowalska finally entered the convent, becoming a postulant on the eve of the Feast of Our Lady of the Angels, August 1, 1925. Later, she wrote: "I felt immensely happy; it seemed to me that I had stepped into the life of Paradise. A single prayer was bursting forth from my heart, one of thanksgiving" (*Diary*, 17).

LIFE IS FULL OF STRUGGLES

But within three weeks, she was tempted to see Mother Superior and leave the community. The lack of time for prayer and the busy work schedule made Helen consider joining a stricter order. But the Lord intervened with a vision of His face in agony. Helen asked, "Jesus, who has hurt you so?" and Jesus answered, **It is you who will cause Me this pain if you leave this convent. It is to this place that I called you and nowhere else; and I have prepared many graces for you** (*Diary*, 19).

During her first year at the convent, Helen's health began to decline, and the Superior sent her away for a rest. Later, along with the other postulants, Helen went to Krakow where the order ran a large institution for wayward girls. There, she finished the remaining three months of her postulancy and prepared to enter the novitiate.

HER YEARS AS A NOVICE

On April 30, 1926, Helen received the habit and veil and her new name, Sr. Maria Faustina of the Most Blessed Sacrament. Later she wrote of the experience in her *Diary*: "The day I took the [religious] habit, God let me understand how much I was to suffer. I clearly saw to what I was committing myself.

I experienced a moment of that suffering. But then God filled my soul again with great consolations" (22).

In Krakow, Sr. Faustina began her two novitiate years of formal training in the work and spiritual life of the community. She was popular with the other novices. Faustina's good nature, willingness to defer to others for the sake of Jesus, and enlightening conversations drew them to her. Toward the end of her first year, she began to experience some of the suffering and struggle that became part of her life and mission. Finding neither joy nor consolation in prayer, and increasingly aware of her own sinfulness, she entered into a dark night of the soul:

> Toward the end of the first year of my novitiate, darkness began to cast its shadow over my soul. I felt no consolation in prayer; I had to make a great effort to meditate; fear began to sweep over me. Going deeper into myself, I could find nothing but great misery. I could also clearly see the great holiness of God. I did not dare to raise my eyes to Him, but reduced myself to dust under His feet and begged for mercy. ... The simple truths of the faith become incomprehensible to me. My soul was in anguish, unable to find comfort anywhere.

> At a certain point, there came to me the very powerful impression that I am rejected by God. This terrible thought pierced my soul right through; in the midst of the suffering my soul began to experience the agony of death. I wanted to die but could not. ... When I made this known to the Directress of Novices, I received this reply, "Know, dear Sister, that God has chosen you for great sanctity. This is a sign that God wants to have you very close to Himself in Heaven. Have great trust in the Lord Jesus" (*Diary*, 23).

Faustina's response to this dark night gives us the key to her spirituality and mission in the Church:

During these terrible moments I said to God, "Jesus, who in the Gospel compare Yourself to a most tender mother, I trust in Your words because You are Truth and Life. In spite of everything, Jesus, I trust in You in the face of every interior sentiment which sets itself against hope. Do what You want with me; I will never leave You, because You are the source of my life" (*Diary*, 24).

Near the end of her novitiate, Faustina's interior sufferings were accompanied by physical weaknesses. The Mother Directress excused her from the customary spiritual disciplines and suggested that Faustina replace them with short prayers. On Good Friday in 1928, Faustina wrote of her experience as she prayed:

> Jesus catches up my heart into the very flame of His love. This was during the evening adoration. All of a sudden, the Divine Presence invaded me, and I forgot everything else. Jesus gave me to understand how much He had suffered for me. This lasted a very short time. An intense yearning — a longing to love God (*Diary*, 26).

FIRST VOWS

Sister Faustina's novitiate ended on April 30, 1928, when she made simple (temporary) vows for one year. The dark night lingered for six more months. Through these sufferings, Faustina grew into a deeper love of the Lord and an awareness of her own misery and God's mercy. She wrote:

> At the beginning of my religious life, suffering and adversities frightened and disheartened me. So I prayed continuously, asking Jesus to strengthen me and to grant me the power of His Holy Spirit that I might carry out His holy will in all things, because from the beginning I have been aware of my weakness. ... The

knowledge of my own misery allows me, at the same time, to know the immensity of Your mercy. In my own interior life, I am looking with one eye at the abyss of my misery and baseness, and with the other, at the abyss of Your mercy, O God (*Diary*, 56).

Six months after making her simple vows, Faustina was assigned to the convent in Warsaw where she had begun her journey into religious life. After just a month of kitchen duty, she became ill and was sent to the infirmary. At this time and throughout much of her life, Faustina suffered not only physically and from her interior struggle but also from harsh treatment by those around her. Many did not believe she was sick but thought she was pretending in order to avoid the rigors of religious life. The distrust and gossip pained her deeply.

Mother Michael, who had admitted Faustina years ago and who had since been elected Superior General of the community, told her: "Sister, along your path, sufferings just spring up out of the ground. I look upon you, Sister, as one crucified. But I can see that Jesus has a hand in this. Be faithful to the Lord" (*Diary*, 149).

Faustina remained faithful through the dull routine of her jobs as she was assigned to different houses. She was sometimes a cook or gardener, and a porter when she was too ill for physical work. In her *Diary*, she reflected on the blessings that even monotonous work could bring:

O life so dull and monotonous, how many treasures you contain! When I look at everything with the eyes of faith, no two hours are alike, and the dullness and monotony disappear. The grace which is given me in this hour will not be repeated in the next (62).

Because of her ready and agreeable nature, Faustina was a blessing to her superiors. They could send her wherever a need arose. They were unaware of her chronic tubercular condition that was aggravated by their demanding assignments.

In June 1930, Sr. Faustina was sent to Plock and Guardian Angel Home, where she was again assigned to kitchen duty. After a few months, the work became too physically demanding. Faustina was sent to the sisters' rest home in Biala, where she remained for the rest of the year. Once she felt better, she returned to Guardian Angel Home to work in the bakery and store. Plock would remain her home until she returned to Warsaw to prepare for perpetual vows in November 1932.

Throughout her years at Plock, Faustina was continually afflicted by illness and spiritual torment. She had found no spiritual director, and her confessors were often unable to help her. Many of her companions thought her strange. The doubts of others sowed doubt in her own heart. However, whenever she spoke to Jesus about her uncertainty or her inability to go on, He reassured her: **Do not fear; I am with you** (*Diary*, 129). In God's plan, this suffering and doubt perfected her trust and the obedience necessary for a mission that would prove far more demanding.

DEVOTIONS OF DIVINE MERCY (1930-38)

THE IMAGE OF THE DIVINE MERCY

The mission of St. Faustina began with a revelation on February 22, 1931, in the convent in Plock. She wrote:

> In the evening, when I was in my cell, I saw the Lord Jesus clothed in a white garment. One hand [was] raised in the gesture of blessing, the other was touching the garment at the breast. From beneath the garment, slightly drawn aside at the breast, there

were emanating two large rays, one red, the other pale. In silence I kept my gaze fixed on the Lord; my soul was struck with awe, but also with great joy. After a while, Jesus said to me, **Paint an image according to the pattern you see with the signature: Jesus, I trust in You. I desire that this image be venerated, first in your chapel, and [then] throughout the world** (*Diary*, 470).

I promise that the soul that will venerate this image will not perish. I also promise victory over [its] enemies already here on earth, especially at the hour of death. I Myself will defend it as My own glory (*Diary*, 48).

This was the first major revelation of Divine Mercy to Sr. Faustina. Through it, Jesus made known His great desire that all come to the rays of mercy, all come to His Heart, pierced for us and flowing with blood and water (see Jn 19:34).

Some time later, her spiritual director and confessor, Fr. Michael Sopocko, told Sr. Faustina to ask the Lord Jesus the meaning of the two rays in the image. Obediently, she recorded His response:

During prayer I heard these words within me: **The two rays denote Blood and Water. The pale ray stands for the Water which makes souls righteous. The red ray stands for the Blood which is the life of souls. ...**

These two rays issued forth from the very depths of My tender mercy when My agonized Heart was opened by a lance on the Cross.

These rays shield souls from the wrath of My Father. Happy is the one who will dwell in their shelter, for the just hand of God shall not lay hold of him (*Diary*, 299).

THE FEAST

Her first revelation was immediately followed by another major request by our Lord for a Feast of Mercy:

> When I told this to my confessor, I received this for a reply: "That refers to your soul." He told me, "Certainly, paint God's image in your soul." When I came out of the confessional, I again heard words such as these: **My image already is in your soul. I desire that there be a Feast of Mercy. I want this image, which you will paint with a brush, to be solemnly blessed on the first Sunday after Easter; that Sunday is to be the Feast of Mercy** (*Diary*, 49).

> **I desire that priests proclaim this great mercy of Mine towards souls of sinners. Let the sinner not be afraid to approach Me. The flames of mercy are burning Me — clamoring to be spent; I want to pour them out upon these souls** (*Diary*, 50).

Soon after these revelations, Faustina suffered increased derision from the sisters. She bore her sufferings in silence. The humiliations and suffering increased. Confused, she sometimes tried to ignore the inspirations by giving her attention more completely to tasks at hand. She prayed for a spiritual director to help her discern God's movement within her soul.

PREPARING FOR FINAL VOWS

In November 1932, Faustina returned to Warsaw to begin her third probation (a period of testing and trial) and to prepare for her perpetual vows. Shortly after arriving, the Mother Directress sent her to a retreat in Walendow. Jesus assured Faustina that during the retreat, He would remove her doubts regarding His commands. This was accomplished through the words of Rev. Edmund Elter, SJ, the retreat master. During her confession, Faustina was reassured that God was the source of her inspirations. Father Elter encouraged her to pray for a spiritual director. Meanwhile, he said, she was to remain faithful to Jesus despite the hardships that would bring to her.

On December 1, 1932, her third probation began. During this year, she continued to have visions and conversations with Jesus in her heart. He was preparing Faustina to make an offering of herself in atonement for the sins of the world. He made it clear to her that she would suffer and that He waited for her free consent. She recorded this in her *Diary*:

> Once during an adoration, the Lord demanded that I give myself up to Him as an offering, by bearing a certain suffering in atonement, not only for the sins of the world in general, but specifically for transgressions committed in this house. Immediately I said, "Very good; I am ready." But Jesus gave me to see what I was going to suffer, and in one moment the whole passion unfolded itself before my eyes. ... All these things stood before my soul's eye like a dark storm from which lightning was ready to strike at any moment, waiting only for my consent. For a moment, my nature was frightened. Then suddenly the dinner bell rang. I left the chapel, trembling and undecided. But the sacrifice was ever present before me, for I had neither decided to accept it, nor had I refused the Lord. I wanted to place myself completely in His will. If the Lord Jesus Himself were to impose it on me, I was ready. But Jesus gave me to know that I myself was to give my free consent and accept it with full consciousness, or else it would be meaningless. Its whole power was contained in my free act before God. ... And so I then answered immediately, "Jesus, I accept everything that You wish to send me; I trust in Your goodness." At that moment, I felt that by this act I glorified God greatly. But I armed myself with patience. As soon as I left the chapel, I had an encounter with reality. I do not want to describe the details, but there was as much of it as I was able to bear (*Diary*, 190).

During Lent, Faustina received the stigmata. She suffered internally from the wounds of Jesus. While no outward sign of Jesus' wounds was present, she felt the agony of them in her hands, feet, and side. This suffering and union with the Passion of Jesus occurred many times throughout her professed life. Since nothing was outwardly visible, only she and her confessor were aware of it. The Mother Directress Margaret, who recognized that God was calling Faustina to a deep union, was a great support to her. Still haunted by doubts, Faustina received Jesus' promise that He would give her help during the retreat before her final profession.

The retreat began on April 17 at St. Joseph's in Krakow. The help came from Fr. Joseph Andrasz, SJ. On the fourth day of the retreat, Faustina confessed to Fr. Andrasz and asked him to release her from her inner visions and the responsibilities they brought. He would not but affirmed her visions and asked her to pray for a permanent spiritual director. Faustina did pray, and she received a vision of her future spiritual director.

FINAL VOWS

On May 1, 1933, Faustina made her perpetual vows as a sister in the Congregation of the Sisters of Our Lady of Mercy. Her joy was beyond expression. In her *Diary*, she wrote that she was nervous about leaving the novitiate and the ever watchful care of Mother Directress. Faustina told Jesus that she would enter His novitiate and remain forever "The little novice of Jesus" (*Diary*, 228).

After her profession, she was sent to Vilnius where she was to become head gardener. With little knowledge of gardening, she trusted God to help her in her work. She was hesitant to leave Fr. Andrasz, but Jesus assured her: **Do not fear. I will not leave you alone.** When she arrived on May 25, 1933, she found a place quite different than St. Joseph's. The convent consisted of a few small huts occupied by 18 sisters. Here, at last, she found her spiritual director, Rev. Michael Sopocko, who was beatified on September 28, 2008. She recognized him from her vision. He was sensitive to her deep spirituality from the first and remained so for the rest of her life. At his direction, she began to write her now famous *Diary*.

During her three years at Vilnius, Faustina remained cheerful, obedient, and patient. The garden thrived, and those with whom she worked noted her saintly behavior.

After Faustina told Fr. Sopocko about Jesus' desire to have an image of her vision of Him painted, the priest arranged for a local artist, Eugene Kazimirowski, to do the work. It began on January 2, 1934. Every two weeks, Sr. Faustina went to him and directed the painting. It was completed in June of that year.

Faustina grew in wisdom and in her love of God. On Holy Thursday, March 29, 1934, Jesus spoke to her, and she responded with an offering of prayer.

> Jesus said to me, **I desire that you make an offering of yourself for sinners and especially for those souls who have lost hope in God's mercy** (*Diary*, 308).

In her prayer "God and Souls: Act of Oblation," Faustina offered herself to God for the conversion of sinners, especially those who had lost hope in God's mercy.

After having made this prayer with the permission of Fr. Sopocko, Sr. Faustina felt immediate results. Her soul "became like a stone — dried up, filled with torment and disquiet" (*Diary*, 311). Still, she accepted all as God's will. The Lord brought Sr. Faustina to a total trust in Him.

Her year continued as usual, filled with work and prayer and punctuated by illness. In August, she suffered her first violent attack of asthma. This may have resulted from the tuberculosis that already plagued her and would cause almost constant suffering for the rest of her life. She continued to have visions of Jesus. In her *Diary*, she recorded experiences and conversations with Him. When she experienced spiritual dryness, as she did during Advent of that year, He reassured her with words of encouragement and a sense of peace.

In February 1935, having received news of her mother's impending death and her wish to see her daughter one last time, Faustina received permission to visit her family. She had not been home for 10 years. Faustina arrived and went directly to her mother. After greeting her with the words, "Praised be Jesus Christ," and assuring Faustina that she would be "up and about," her mother sat up in bed. While her doctors had told her she could not improve without surgery, Faustina's mother was well. In fact, she lived to be 90!

Friends and neighbors filled the house and brought their children for Faustina to hold and kiss. The guests enjoyed hearing her tell stories of the saints and speak of God. While she enjoyed the visit and gave thanks for the opportunity to see her family again, she missed solitude and prayer. On her return to the convent, Jesus assured her that her time with her family had been pleasing to him.

During Lent, Jesus revealed to her that the image of The Divine Mercy should be publicly displayed and venerated. Despite his doubts about being able to arrange it, and at considerable personal expense, Fr. Sopocko had the painting displayed in a prominent window of the Ostra Brama (the Shrine of Our Lady of Mercy in Vilnius). He preached there at the three-day celebration at the end of the Jubilee Year of Redemption, 1935. This first display of the image fell on the Feast of Divine Mercy.

Faustina soon received a message from Jesus that would trouble her for most of her remaining years: He asked that she leave her congregation and begin a new community. Time after time, she asked her spiritual director and her confessors about this. Each time she was told to wait, or not to do anything without the consent of her superiors. Faustina loved her community and was not eager to leave it. However, she would do anything if she knew it was God's will.

Some people believe that this prophetic sense of Faustina being called to found a community was fulfilled when Fr. Sopocko founded the Congregation of Sisters of the Merciful Jesus in Vilnius in 1941, three years after her death.

THE CHAPLET

In September 1935, God revealed to her a powerful prayer for mercy on the whole world: the Chaplet of Divine Mercy. Said on the beads of the rosary, the prayer pleads for God's mercy on the world, offering Him the sacrifice of His beloved Son, Jesus Christ. Later, Fr. Sopocko had this prayer printed on a holy card with the image of The Divine Mercy reproduced on the opposite side.

The chaplet, the Act of Oblation, the abandonment to God's will, the stigmata, and her close identification with Jesus' Passion all point to Faustina's role in the Church. On September 30, Faustina wrote in her *Diary* that she was sure of her mission to the Church and the world: She was to spend her life pleading for mercy for the world.

How that would be accomplished she was not sure. During her October retreat in Krakow, she asked her confessor, Fr. Andrasz, about forming the new community. Again, he advised against doing anything at that time. He felt Faustina's perpetual vows were a sign that God wanted her to remain in her present congregation. If she remained faithful to God and obedient to her superiors, Fr. Andrasz reassured her, the Lord would not allow her to fall into error. In later visions, Jesus also comforted her. His will would be done. She should not worry about how it would come about.

Try as she might, Faustina could not put worry over the new community out of her heart. On one hand, it seemed that Jesus was telling her to begin something new. On the other, her superiors and confessors continued to discourage immediate action. This spiritual turmoil affected her physical health. She approached the Archbishop of Vilnius, Romuald Jalbrzykowski, at the beginning of 1936 to ask his guidance. He added his voice to the others: Wait.

After a visit to Warsaw in March 1936, Faustina accepted a new assignment to a convent in Walendow. The convent was financially unstable, and the sisters were required to work long hours. Despite her poor health, Faustina was assigned difficult tasks. Her health worsened, and in late April, she was sent to Derdy, a country home for girls. Located in the forest near Walendow, it provided Faustina a place to rest and pray. However, her health continued to decline. On May 11, she returned to Warsaw, where she would be closer to doctors.

Faustina continued to have visions and conversations with Jesus. Her physical and spiritual sufferings increased, but she bore them with patience and love. Joining her sufferings to the sufferings of Jesus was her way of obtaining mercy for souls and for the world.

In September, the Blessed Virgin Mary appeared to her and asked her to pray especially for Poland. Also, in this month, Faustina received a message about the Feast of Divine Mercy. Jesus told her that He desired it to be celebrated on the first Sunday after Easter. On that day, He would pour out an "ocean of graces" (*Diary*, 699). He promised complete forgiveness of sins and of punishment to anyone who would make a good confession beforehand and receive Holy Communion on that feast.

Faustina faithfully recorded all Jesus said to her. Her suffering increased, and at the end of the month, her illness was diagnosed as tuberculosis. She was separated from the other sisters to avoid spreading the disease. However, she still had chores to do.

On her October retreat, she experienced union with God and had a vision of hell. She was also told explicit ways to worship the mercy of God: First, she must show mercy, which grows from love of God, to all her neighbors. Second, she was to show such mercy in three ways: in deed, word, and prayer.

HER ILLNESS WORSENS

Finally, in December of 1936, Faustina was sent to the sanatorium in Pradnik, near Krakow, for three months of treatments. She had a private room and was treated with great kindness. As sick as she was, Faustina found strength to minister to other sick and dying patients. Sometimes she would waken in the night, knowing that someone was near death and in need of prayer. As Jesus had instructed her, she prayed the Chaplet of Divine Mercy, obtaining for the person a peaceful death and the unlimited mercy of God.

Much to her delight, Faustina was permitted to return home to her convent to celebrate Christmas. She enjoyed her few days with her community, but by December 27, she was back at the sanatorium.

When the New Year 1937 arrived, Faustina resolved to do all she could to grow in holiness and attain union with God. She tried to do what she imagined He would do in every situation. Jesus assured her that above all she must love her neighbor and think first of others. As time went on, Faustina felt less at home on earth and longed for the day when she would be united with her Lord for eternity.

Lent was a time of special graces for Faustina. Then, on Good Friday, she was completely immersed in the Trinity. On Holy Saturday, she was able to return to the convent in Lagiewniki, near Krakow. There, Jesus appeared to her at Easter Mass.

However, despite her growing union with God and the many graces she received, Faustina remained concerned about her inability to complete the work of God that she felt called to do: Begin a new community. When the Mother General visited the convent to receive the sisters' vows, Faustina asked her again about leaving. Mother told her that whatever she chose to do, she could do. When Faustina left the meeting, a feeling of great darkness wrapped itself about her. When she confided that to Mother General, she was told that her desire to leave was a great temptation. Faustina called this dilemma an "endless agony of the soul" (*Diary*, 1116).

Throughout the spring and summer, Faustina continued to record Jesus' words to her. She was told that we most resemble God when we forgive one another. God is Love, Mercy, and Goodness. She found following Jesus difficult but never lost her desire to be a mirror of her beloved Lord.

At the end of July, Faustina was moved to Rabka, a village in the Carpathian Mountains. There, she stayed in a rest home for girls and sisters. Her lungs were excruciatingly painful, and her health continued to worsen. She was visited with visions of Mary, Joseph, and St. Barbara. On August 10, she returned to Krakow, where she wrote down the Novena to The Divine Mercy. Father Sopocko visited her at the end of the month and told her that work on establishing a Feast of Divine Mercy was going well, as were his efforts to spread the chaplet, litany, and novena.

At Mass on the First Friday of September, having made a prayer of total abandonment to God's will, Faustina had reached a stage of holy indifference. She trusted in God completely, willing to accept whatever He required of her.

Much suffering was in store for her. Despite physical agony, Faustina still had assigned duties at the convent. Only Jesus knew the effort required to perform them. Another source of anguish came from the unkindness and suspicions of those with whom she lived. Her life was a confirmation of the letter she received from Fr. Sopocko: God required prayer and sacrifice from her. Her work would be suffering, not the action of forming a new community.

HER FINAL YEAR

Her last year, 1938, began as the old one had ended: with physical and spiritual pain. She welcomed the New Year, however, and all it would bring. She saw its increased suffering as more opportunities to love God and save souls. Since Jesus had revealed to her the day of her death, she knew that it, too, was coming in the New Year. She was more than ready to embrace it.

In her bleakest times, Jesus consoled her, saying that He was with her, even when she could not feel His presence. She continued to write and to accept without complaining the cruel treatment she received from those who were her caretakers. The year was filled with times of darkness when she was confused and had to make a willful choice to believe.

During this time, as in every part of her life, Faustina found comfort in the Holy Eucharist. When others demanded more of her than she could physically do, she depended on Jesus' strength, given through the Blessed Sacrament, to sustain her. When she was too ill to attend Mass, she would make her way there for Holy Communion. When she was too ill for that, others brought Holy Communion to her. During her last, long stay at the sanatorium, when no one could bring her the Host, she received Holy Communion from the hands of an angel.

Faustina returned to the sanatorium in April. She was well cared for, and while there, she ministered to others as she was able by listening, prayer, and counsel. By June, Sr. Faustina was too ill to write in her *Diary*. During her last weeks, she struggled to complete her final notebook. She knew the message of mercy would spread over the whole world.

At the end of August, Faustina wrote a letter to Mother Michael, the Mother General. Faustina thanked her for all she had done, for the graces received from the community, and asked forgiveness for any offenses she had committed.

Faustina's condition grew worse. On August 25, her 33rd birthday, she received the Anointing of the Sick. Father Sopocko visited her on August 28 and again on September 2. After taking his leave, he remembered something he had left and returned to her room. He found her in ecstasy and did not disturb her.

On September 17, she was taken home to the convent to die. She lay in a private room, unable to eat. Five days later, according to custom, she formally asked pardon of the entire community. On September 29, Fr. Sopocko made his last visit.

Finally, on October 5, Fr. Andrasz heard her last confession. For much of the evening, she was surrounded by the sisters and the chaplain. After they left, at 10:45 p.m., the one sister who had remained with her ran to summon the others. Sister Faustina of the Most Blessed Sacrament looked to heaven and died, united at last with her beloved Jesus.

Her funeral Mass was held on October 7. Not wanting her family to bear the expense and suffering, Faustina had not informed them of her final illness. They were not present at her funeral. After the Mass, her coffin was carried to the common grave of the community, and there she was buried. As Faustina herself predicted, her work on earth had just begun. She would leave a lasting mission of mercy.

CHAPTER 2

❖❖❖❖❖

The Mission of St. Faustina

Although her mission as a professed sister was obedience to her superiors, our Lord also called Faustina to a special mission: She was to be His apostle of Divine Mercy, proclaiming God's limitless mercy to the world by example and by faithfully recording His revelations. "Glorifying Your mercy," she wrote, "is the exclusive task of my life" (*Diary*, 1242).

Throughout her life, she grew in understanding this call. Faustina developed deep humility through obedience to the will of God as expressed through her superiors and her spiritual directors. She conscientiously kept a spiritual diary as Fr. Sopocko requested. Trusting in God's sustaining grace, she entered fully into the Passion of Jesus. Eventually, she offered herself completely, especially her sufferings and her prayers, for the salvation of souls.

REVELATIONS

Faustina was just seven when she first heard Jesus speaking in her soul, and such revelations continued for the rest of her life. Some revelations advised Faustina how to act in particular situations and how to respond to people around her. Others directed her in the journey to oneness with God.

Through them, God guided Faustina as she faced life's major decisions as well as its dull routines. Whether making known His passionate desire for the salvation of souls, or helping her cope with the physical demands of kitchen duty, Jesus was always present to her. The most famous of Faustina's revelations have to do with Divine Mercy. The first was of the image of the merciful Savior, under the title of The Divine Mercy, now recognized throughout the world. The revelation that has greatest significance for the whole Church is the Feast of Divine Mercy, which is now known as Divine

Mercy Sunday. Sister Faustina recorded the desire of the Lord for this feast at the time of the original revelation of the image and at 14 other times:

> My daughter, tell the whole world about My inconceivable mercy, I desire that the Feast of Mercy be a refuge and shelter for all souls, especially for poor sinners. On that day the very depths of My tender mercy are open. I pour out a whole ocean of graces upon those souls who approach the fount of My mercy. ... Let no soul fear to draw near to Me, even though its sins be as scarlet. My mercy is so great that no mind, be it of man or of angel, will be able to fathom it throughout all eternity (*Diary*, 699).

In response to these messages, at the time of his canonization of Faustina on April 30, 2000, Pope John Paul II proclaimed the first Sunday after Easter as Divine Mercy Sunday for the universal Church.

In another revelation, Jesus taught Faustina a special prayer, the Chaplet of Divine Mercy:

> This prayer will serve to appease My wrath. You will recite it for nine days, on the beads of the rosary, in the following manner: First of all, you will say one OUR FATHER and HAIL MARY and the I BELIEVE IN GOD. Then on the OUR FATHER beads you will say the following words: "Eternal Father, I offer You the Body and Blood, Soul and Divinity of Your dearly beloved Son, Our Lord Jesus Christ, in atonement for our sins and those of the whole world." On the HAIL MARY beads you will say the following words: "For the sake of His sorrowful Passion, have mercy on us and on the whole world." In conclusion, three times you will recite these words: "Holy God,

Holy Mighty One, Holy Immortal One, have mercy on us and on the whole world" (*Diary*, 476).

Jesus told Faustina that He would grant the requests of those who recited this prayer. Sinners who prayed it would be filled with peace and would have a happy death. He especially encouraged Faustina to pray it at the bedside of the dying:

Write that when they say this chaplet in the presence of the dying, I will stand between My Father and the dying person, not as the just Judge but as the merciful Savior (*Diary*, 1541).

PREPARATION FOR HER MISSION

In order to carry out her mission of redemptive suffering for the salvation of sinners and focus the world's attention on the mercy of God, Faustina gave herself unreservedly to Jesus. She trusted that He would prepare her for her work and sustain her as she strove to remain faithful to His call.

Indeed, Jesus was her Teacher. She wrote:

I would not know how to live without the Lord. Jesus often visits me in this seclusion, teaches me, reassures me, rebukes me, and admonishes me. He Himself forms my heart according to His divine wishes and likings, but always with much goodness and mercy (*Diary*, 1024).

Faustina learned well to respond to His invitation in the Gospel: "Come to Me, all you who labor and are burdened, and I will give you rest. Take My yoke upon you and learn from Me, for I am meek and humble of heart; and you will find rest for yourselves. For My yoke is easy and My burden light" (Mt 11:28-30).

She was given the ability to see every moment of life as an opportunity to share the Lord's yoke and to deepen her relationship with God. Even routine chores and the taunts of other sisters became sources of grace. Jesus encouraged her:

> **I was your Teacher, I am and I will be; strive to make your heart like unto My humble and gentle Heart. Never claim your rights. Bear with great calm and patience everything that befalls you. Do not defend yourself when you are put to shame, though innocent. Let others triumph. Do not stop being good when you notice that your goodness is being abused. I Myself will speak up for you when it is necessary** (*Diary*, 1701).

Later, she would write:

> I accept joy or suffering, praise or humiliation with the same disposition. I remember that one and the other are passing. What does it matter to me what people say about me? I have long ago given up everything that concerns my person. My name is host — or sacrifice, not in words but in deeds, in the emptying of myself and in becoming like You on the Cross, O good Jesus, my Master! (*Diary*, 485).

Jesus helped her deal not only with emotional anguish but also with intense physical suffering that plagued Faustina for much of her adult life. Tuberculosis and its complications made completion of assigned chores difficult. Despite tremendous human effort, they sometimes were accomplished only with divine help. Exhaustion and weakness required Faustina to rest, and she spent time in convent infirmaries and in a sanatorium. These periods of rest often invited resentment and cruel remarks from those around her.

SPIRITUAL TRIALS

Illness was not Faustina's only source of physical suffering. She also experienced agonizing pain from an internal stigmata (see *Diary*, 964). While this was not constant, it recurred often during her life. As with all afflictions, she willingly embraced it as a means of gaining sanctity. She learned that suffering was God's gift to her:

> Suffering is a great grace; through suffering the soul becomes like the Savior; in suffering love becomes crystallized; the greater the suffering, the purer the love (*Diary*, 67).

Jesus purified her soul through spiritual trials as well. The dark night that Faustina experienced early in her religious life was one such crucible. Only after she had passed through it, did she recognize it for what it was:

> After such sufferings the soul finds itself in a state of great purity of spirit and very close to God. But I should add that during these spiritual torments it is close to God, but it is blind. The soul's vision is plunged into darkness, and though God is nearer than ever to the soul which is suffering, the whole secret consists in the fact that it knows nothing of this. The soul in fact declares that, not only has God abandoned it, but it is the object of His hatred. ... Yet despite all, I learned later that God is closer to a soul at such moments than at others, because it would not be able to endure these trials with the help of ordinary grace alone. God's omnipotence and an extraordinary grace must be active here, for otherwise the soul would succumb at the first blow (*Diary*, 109).

Another spiritual trial was the push and pull of confusion about founding a new congregation. Jesus asked her to do so, but she met resistance at every turn. The matter was a constant source of distress for Faustina. Yet her struggles helped to deepen her complete trust in Jesus.

Nurturing this trust, Jesus sustained Faustina in two other important ways. First, he provided her with a spiritual director, a confessor, and superiors who were sensitive to her unique spiritual journey. Open to God's grace, they all responded to Faustina in ways that helped her along her path to holiness. Jesus admonished her to be obedient to them in all things. Through them, He guided His eager pupil along her way, making sure she would not fall into error or be misled.

She wrote of the two priests in her *Diary*:

> But my torments are coming to an end. The Lord is giving me the promised help. I can see it in two priests; namely, Father Andrasz and Father Sopocko. During the retreat before my perpetual vows, I was set completely at peace for the first time [by Father Andrasz], and afterwards I was led in the same direction by Father Sopocko. This was the fulfillment of the Lord's promise (*Diary*, 141).

MOTTO OF ST. FAUSTINA: 'GOD AND SOULS'

The motto of St. Faustina "God and Souls" appears 11 times in her *Diary*. In fact, this motto is among the first words in the first three notebooks of the *Diary*. The motto is special to St. Faustina because it summarizes her mission of mercy as all for God's glory and the salvation of souls. Further, this motto brings into focus the value of suffering in fulfilling her mission. As she writes in one passage:

> During Holy Mass, I saw the Lord Jesus nailed upon the cross amidst great torments. A soft moan issued from His Heart. After some time, He said, **I thirst. I thirst for the salvation of souls. Help Me, My daughter to save souls. Join your sufferings to My Passion and offer them to the heavenly Father for sinners** (*Diary*, 1032).

Keeping this aim of "God and Souls" uppermost in mind helped St. Faustina appreciate the true value of suffering:

> Oh, if only the suffering soul knew how it is loved by God, it would die of joy and excess of happiness! Some day, we will know the value of suffering, but then we will no longer be able to suffer, The present moment is ours (*Diary*, 963).

Saint Faustina also shows us the power of such suffering for God and souls, as she takes on the suffering of her confessor and spiritual director, Blessed Fr. Michael Sopocko. As she bore his suffering, the Lord revealed to her what Fr. Sopocko himself would have to suffer in fulfilling his own mission:

> Once, a certain priest [Father Sopocko] asked me to pray for him. I promised to pray, and asked for a mortification. When I received permission for a certain mortification, I felt a great desire to give up all the graces that God's goodness would intend for me that day in favor of that priest, and I asked the Lord Jesus to deign to bestow on me all the sufferings and afflictions, both exterior and spiritual, that the priest would have had to suffer during that day. God partially answered my request and, at once, all sorts of difficulties and adversities sprang up out of nowhere, so much so that one of the sisters remarked out loud that the Lord Jesus must have a hand in this because everyone was trying Sister Faustina. The charges made were so groundless that what some sisters put forward, others denied, while I offered all this in silence on behalf of the priest.

> But that was not all; I began to experience interior sufferings. First, I was seized by depression and aversion towards the sisters, then a kind of uncertainty began to trouble me. I could not recollect myself during prayer, and various things would take hold of

my mind. When, tired out, I entered the chapel, a strange pain seized my soul, and I began to weep softly. Then I heard in my soul a voice, saying, **My daughter, why are you weeping? After all, you yourself offered to undertake these sufferings. Know that what you have taken upon yourself for that soul is only a small portion. He is suffering much more.** And I asked the Lord, "Why are You treating him like that?" The Lord answered me that it was for the triple crown meant for him: that of virginity, the priesthood and martyrdom. At that moment, a great joy flooded my soul at the sight of the great glory that is going to be his in heaven. Right away I said the *Te Deum* for this special grace of God; namely, of learning how God treats those He intends to have close to Himself. Thus, all sufferings are nothing in comparison with what awaits us in heaven (*Diary*, 596).

Interestingly, in a footnote to this *Diary* passage, we learn that Fr. Sopocko wrote of this very incident in his memoirs:

[M]y troubles reached their peak in January 1936. I never mentioned them to anyone, and it was only on the critical day that I asked Sr. Faustina for prayer. To my great surprise, all of my troubles vanished into thin air on that day, and Sister Faustina told me she had taken all my sufferings upon herself and experienced so much suffering that day as she never had before (A. SF. Recol.).

Notice how in bearing the suffering of Blessed Fr. Michael Sopocko, St. Faustina experienced a number of spiritual attacks! She experienced all sorts of difficulties, interior sufferings, depression, aversion toward others, troubling uncertainty, inability to pray, fatigue, pain, and weeping. Yet it was worth it all as a means to helping her fellow apostle of Divine Mercy.

This becomes clear when St. Faustina records a further word about Blessed Fr. Michael Sopocko. In fact, I remember reading this powerful text at the tomb of Blessed Michael Sopocko in Bialystok, Poland, on one of my pilgrimages. I was and am deeply impressed by the word of the Lord about this priest being after the Lord's own Heart in fulfilling his mission of mercy:

> [August] 30 [1937]. Reverend Father Sopocko left this morning. When I was steeped in a prayer of thanksgiving for the great grace that I had received from God; namely, that of seeing Father, I became united in a special way with the Lord who said to me, **He is a priest after My own Heart; his efforts are pleasing to Me. You see, My daughter, that My will must be done and that which I had promised you, I shall do. Through him I spread comfort to suffering and careworn souls. Through him it pleased Me to proclaim the worship of My mercy. And through this work of mercy more souls will come close to Me than otherwise would have, even if he had kept giving absolution day and night for the rest of his life, because by so doing, he would have labored only for as long as he lived; whereas, thanks to this work of mercy, he will be laboring till the end of the world** (*Diary*, 1256).

THE HOLY EUCHARIST, THE PRESENCE OF MERCY

Faustina found the strength to bear her sufferings through the Sacraments, particularly the Eucharist and Reconciliation. Faustina had a deep love and need for the Holy Eucharist. She grasped its mystery and relied on its power. She makes these revealing statements about her life:

The most solemn moment of my life is the moment when I receive Holy Communion. I long for each Holy Communion, and for every Holy Communion I give thanks to the Most Holy Trinity (*Diary*, 1804).

All the good that is in me is due to Holy Communion. I owe everything to it. I feel that this holy fire has transformed me completely. Oh, how happy I am to be a dwelling place for You, O Lord! My heart is a temple in which You dwell continually (*Diary*, 1392).

The Holy Eucharist is central to devotion to The Divine Mercy, so much so that Our Lord specifically asks, through Sister Faustina, that we all receive Holy Communion on the Feast of Divine Mercy, after preparing for it through the Sacrament of Reconciliation. In the Eucharist, Jesus (Mercy Incarnate) is present Body and Blood, Soul and Divinity. The Eucharist is God's sacrificial gift of mercy, offered in atonement for our sins and those of the whole world; and in receiving this mercy in Holy Communion, we are strengthened and consoled by the Lord who is Love and Mercy itself.

Pope John Paul II spoke of these three aspects of the Eucharist — presence, sacrifice, and communion — as essential to our understanding of our faith (see his encyclical *Redeemer of Man*). The presence of the Lord calls for our adoration, the sacrifice calls for offering ourselves with Christ, and communion calls us to live in union with Him.

Through her life and writings, Sister Faustina gives us a perfect model for responding to this threefold call of Jesus in the Eucharist; the Eucharist was so central to her life that she referred to it in some way on most of the pages of her *Diary* and wrote 16 beautiful prayers of preparation for Holy Communion.

ADORATION

Sister Faustina's Adoration of the Eucharist began with the recognition of the great mystery of the Mass itself, and she urges us to special reverence and participation:

Oh, what awesome mysteries take place during Mass! A great mystery is accomplished in the Holy Mass. With what great devotion should we listen to and take part in this death of Jesus. One day we will know what God is doing for us in each Mass, and what sort of gift He is preparing in it for us. Only His divine love could permit that such a gift be provided for us (*Diary*, 914).

During her working day, Sister Faustina used every free moment to stop before the Blessed Sacrament and visit the Lord. She also spent special hours of Adoration interceding for other people, especially those lost in sin.

These hours spent before the Blessed Sacrament resulted in a special Litany of Adoration of the Eucharist, which she wrote in 1935, emphasizing the Eucharist as the Mystery of Mercy (see *Diary*, 356).

OFFERING

One year, on Holy Thursday, Sister Faustina saw, in a vision, the institution of the Eucharist in the Cenacle and was given to understand that in the offering that Jesus made of Himself on the night before He died, the sacrifice was fully consummated:

I was most deeply moved when before the Consecration, Jesus raised His eyes to heaven and entered into a mysterious conversation with His Father. It is only in eternity that we shall really understand that moment ... . At the moment of Consecration, love rested satiated — the sacrifice fully consummated. Now only the external ceremony of death will be carried out — external destruction; the essence [of it] is in the Cenacle (*Diary*, 684).

This means then, that the Eucharistic *offering* is the essence of the sacrifice of Jesus. In every Mass, united with the priest, we offer the very Body and Blood, Soul and Divinity of our Lord Jesus Christ, made present on the altar by the words and actions of the priest through the power of the Holy Spirit. We unite the offering of ourselves with His offering, which is already accepted by the Father, and is made present to us here and now.

During Exposition of the Blessed Sacrament and during Mass itself, Sister Faustina regularly saw our Lord. Most often she saw Him as a child; but at times, He appeared with rays of light as in The Divine Mercy image. At other times, she saw Him in His Passion and was able to participate in it with Him, sharing His pain:

> Today [February 2, 1937], from early morning, Divine absorption penetrates my soul. During Mass, I thought I would see the little Jesus, as I often do; however, today during Holy Mass I saw the Crucified Jesus. Jesus was nailed to the cross and was in great agony. His suffering pierced me, soul and body, in a manner which was invisible, but nevertheless most painful (*Diary*, 913).

UNION

Uniting herself to Jesus through the regular reception of Holy Communion, Sister Faustina learned to draw all her strength and consolation from the Eucharist, a lesson that is important for us to learn as well. She writes of this reality:

> One thing alone sustains me, and that is Holy Communion. From it I draw my strength; in it is all my comfort … . Jesus concealed in the Host is everything to me. From the tabernacle I draw strength, power, courage, and light. Here, I seek consolation in time of anguish. I would not know how to give glory to God if I did not have the Eucharist in my heart (*Diary*, 1037).

As the battle of each day began, she found renewed confidence and strength in the Eucharist. It gave her the grace she needed to fulfill her mission:

Every morning during meditation, I prepare myself for the whole day's struggle. Holy Communion assures me that I will win the victory; and so it is … . This Bread of the Strong gives me all the strength I need to carry on my mission and the courage to do whatever the Lord asks of me. The courage and strength that are in me are not of me, but of Him who lives in me — it is the Eucharist (*Diary*, 91).

She learned, too, that the Lord continued to live in her — continued to be present in her, as in a tabernacle — until her next reception of the Eucharist in Holy Communion:

Today, I have come to understand many of God's mysteries. I have come to know that Holy Communion remains in me until the next Holy Communion. A vivid and clearly felt presence of God continues in my soul. The awareness of this plunges me into deep recollection, without the slightest effort on my part. My heart is a living tabernacle in which the living Host is reserved. I have never sought God in some far-off place, but within myself. It is in the depths of my own being that I commune with my God (*Diary*, 1302, September 29, 1937).

On more than one occasion, the Lord shared with her how closely He wants to unite Himself with us through the Eucharist, if only we would recognize and value His Real Presence in Holy Communion:

My great delight is to unite Myself with souls. … [W]hen I come to a human heart in Holy Communion, My hands are full of all kinds of graces which I want to give to the soul. But souls do not even pay any attention to Me; they leave Me to Myself and busy themselves with other things. Oh, how sad I am that souls do not recognize Love! They treat Me as a dead object (*Diary*, 1385).

Sister Faustina's recognition of Christ's Real Presence in the Eucharist and her unconditional "yes" to His call for sacrifice and unity should be an inspiration to us all to reexamine our own response to this great Sacrament, in which the Lord of mercy pours Himself into our hearts. Such a recognition of Jesus' Eucharistic presence sustained her throughout the day:

> I often feel God's presence after Holy Communion in a special and tangible way. I know God is in my heart. And the fact that I feel Him in my heart does not interfere with my duties. Even when I am dealing with very important matters which require attention, I do not lose the presence of God in my soul, and I am closely united with Him. With Him, I go to work, with Him I go for recreation, with Him I suffer, with Him I rejoice; I live in Him and He in me. I am never alone, because He is my constant companion. He is present to me at every moment (*Diary*, 318).

RECONCILIATION: TRIBUNAL OF MERCY

Since we are weak human beings and we do sin ("even the just man falls seven times a day"), the Lord has provided a Sacrament of Mercy through which He forgives us and heals us when we fall and are wounded. He spoke repeatedly to Sister Faustina about the Sacrament of Reconciliation as a "Tribunal of Mercy," wherein we receive a judgment, not of condemnation, but of love when we turn back to Him and sincerely repent of our sins. Our Lord made it clear to her that we don't have to make "a great pilgrimage" or perform some other act in order to receive the miracle of Divine Mercy, which can be found in the confessional:

Tell souls where they are to look for solace; that is, in the Tribunal of Mercy [the Sacrament of Reconciliation]. **There the greatest miracles take place** [and] **are incessantly repeated. To avail oneself of this miracle, it is not necessary to go on a great pilgrimage or to carry out some external ceremony; it suffices to come with faith to the feet of My representative and to reveal to him one's misery, and the miracle of Divine Mercy will be fully demonstrated** (*Diary*, 1448).

The Sacrament of Reconciliation became a regular and important part of Sr. Faustina's life, and she grew in her understanding of it. She learned that confession is much more than just asking for and receiving forgiveness. "We should derive two kinds of profit from Holy Confession," she explained: "1. We come to Confession to be healed; 2. We come to be educated — like a small child, our soul has constant need of education" (*Diary*, 377).

She realized that this need of our souls for education — through the grace of God and through the guidance of a good confessor — is vital to our spiritual growth. We cannot simply rely on ourselves:

[O]n its own strength, the soul will not go far; it will exert itself greatly and will do nothing for the glory of God; it will err continually, because our mind is darkened and does not know how to discern its own affairs (*Diary*, 377).

Another important lesson Sister learned was to pray for her confessor:

I came to understand one thing: that I must pray much for each of my confessors, that he might obtain the light of the Holy Spirit, for when I approach the confessional without first praying fervently, the confessor does not understand me very well. Father encouraged me to pray fervently for these intentions, that God would give better knowledge and understanding of the things He is asking of me (*Diary*, 647).

Through Sister Faustina, Christ Himself instructs us how to prepare to receive this great Sacrament of Mercy:

> [W]hen you go to confession, to this fountain of My mercy, the Blood and Water which came forth from My Heart always flows down upon your soul and ennobles it. Every time you go to confession, immerse yourself entirely in My mercy, with great trust, so that I may pour the bounty of My grace upon your soul (*Diary*, 1602).

Repeatedly, the Lord emphasized that the confessional is the place of the greatest mercy, and that it is He, Himself, Mercy Incarnate, who waits for us there. In this light, "the person of the priest" is "only a screen" for Jesus Himself:

> When you approach the confessional, know this, that I Myself am waiting there for you. I am only hidden by the priest, but I Myself act in your soul. Here the misery of the soul meets the God of Mercy (*Diary*, 1602).

> My daughter, just as you prepare in My presence, so also you make your confession before Me. The person of the priest is, for Me, only a screen. Never analyze what sort of a priest it is that I am making use of; open your soul in confession as you would to Me, and I will fill it with My light (*Diary*, 1725).

He stresses, too, that no matter how great our sin, His mercy is greater and can restore us to His grace:

> Were a soul like a decaying corpse so that from a human standpoint, there would be no [hope of] restoration and everything would already be lost,

it is not so with God. The miracle of Divine Mercy restores that soul in full (*Diary*, 1448).

Our sinfulness, then, cannot keep us from receiving His mercy. Only our fear and refusal to trust in Him can block His love. So our Lord urges Sister Faustina:

Pray for souls that they be not afraid to approach the tribunal of My Mercy. Do not grow weary of praying for sinners. … Tell souls that from this fount of mercy souls draw graces solely with the vessel of trust. If their trust is great, there is no limit to My generosity (*Diary*, 975, 1602).

The Church, likewise, continues to exhort us to make frequent use of this Sacrament of Reconciliation, even monthly, to draw on this infinite fount of mercy. Blessed John Paul II had a special concern that we make use of the Sacrament and be healed of one of the great sins of our age — the loss of a sense of sin.

Our Lord emphasized the importance of the Sacrament by making its reception one of the conditions for celebrating the Feast of Mercy:

On that day, the very depths of My tender mercy are open. I pour out a whole ocean of graces upon those souls who approach the Fount of My mercy. The soul that will go to Confession and receive Holy Communion shall obtain complete forgiveness of sins and punishment (*Diary*, 699).

The Sacrament of Reconciliation, in which we confess our sins, is truly a special place for receiving God's mercy. It really is a "Tribunal of Mercy," not one of condemnation, if we but trust in the Lord's mercy and sincerely repent of our sins.

The Sacrament of Reconciliation, the Tribunal of Mercy, became a regular and important part of Faustina's spiritual life, as the Lord prepared her for her mission of mercy. She grew in her understanding of its formative as well as its healing effects on the soul.

LIVING OUT HER MISSION OF MERCY

Along with receiving the great Sacraments of Mercy, Sr. Faustina lived her mission by writing of God's mercy in her *Diary* and by offering everything she did, all her suffering and unceasing prayers, for the salvation of souls. Much of what we know of this comes from her *Diary*.

In 1934, during her stay in Vilnius, Sr. Faustina was told by her confessor, Fr. Sopocko, to write down her interior experiences. When asked by someone in the congregation why Sr. Faustina had been writing a diary, Fr. Sopocko answered: "I was a professor at the Seminary and at the School of Theology of the Stefan Batory University in Vilnius at the time. I had no time to listen to her lengthy confessions at the confessional, so I told her to write everything down and then to show it to me from time to time. This is how the *Diary* came into being" (Fr. Sopocko's letter of March 6, 1972).

In addition to this order from her confessor, Sr. Faustina mentions on many pages of her *Diary* a command to write given her by the Lord Jesus Himself:

> January 23 [1937]. I did not feel like writing today. Then I heard a voice in my soul: **My daughter, you do not live for yourself but for souls; write for their benefit** (*Diary*, 895).

> And Jesus said, **Secretary of My most profound mystery, know that yours is an exclusive intimacy with Me. Your task is to write down everything that I make known to you about My mercy, for the benefit of those who by reading these things will be comforted in their souls and will have the courage to approach Me. I therefore want you to devote all your free moments to writing** (*Diary*, 1693).

Her *Diary* has reached out to the world not only in the original Polish language but also in English, Spanish, Portuguese, Russian, French, Italian, German, and Korean, as well as through partially translated texts in leaflets in dozens of languages. It is numbered among the outstanding works of mystical literature.

Besides writing, Faustina remained faithful to her call by doing all in her power to bring souls to recognize and accept God's gift of mercy. At times, that required her to follow Jesus' spoken commands: She directed the artist as he painted the revealed image of The Divine Mercy. She made known the Chaplet of Divine Mercy, and she encouraged those who were able to work for the establishment of the Feast of Divine Mercy.

Beyond this, Faustina offered every aspect of her life to God for the salvation of souls. Jesus told her that she would save more souls through her prayer and sacrifice than missionaries would through their teaching and sermons. He instructed her to embrace all sufferings with love. The Lord demanded works of mercy from Faustina and taught her how to exercise them:

> **I am giving you three ways of exercising mercy toward your neighbor: the first — by deed, the second — by word, the third — by prayer. In these three degrees is contained the fullness of mercy, and it is an unquestionable proof of love for Me** (*Diary*, 742).

As Faustina strove to live her life as an example of Divine Mercy, she increased her ability to leave her will behind. She abandoned herself to doing the will of God. Her trust in God became absolute. She wrote:

> I firmly trust and commit myself entirely to Your holy will, which is mercy itself (*Diary*, 1574).

> From today onward Your will, Lord, is my food. Lead me, O God, along whatever roads You please; I have placed all my trust in Your will which is, for me, love and mercy itself (*Diary*, 1264).

UNION WITH GOD

We have seen how receiving Jesus regularly in Holy Communion was the key to Sr. Faustina's intimate union with the Lord Jesus. Through the Eucharist and other means, the Lord grants to certain souls, like Faustina's, special graces of union with Himself in order to do some great work that is, humanly speaking, absolutely beyond their power:

> **Know, My daughter, that between Me and you there is a bottomless abyss, an abyss which separates the Creator from the creature. But this abyss is filled with My mercy. I raise you up to Myself, not that I have need of you, but it is solely out of mercy that I grant you the grace of union with Myself** (*Diary*, 1576).

Faustina's union with God empowered her to proclaim His mercy;

> When I entered the chapel, once again the majesty of God overwhelmed me. I felt that I was immersed in God, totally immersed in Him and penetrated by Him, being aware of how much the heavenly Father loves us. Oh, what great happiness fills my heart from knowing God and the divine life! It is my desire to share this happiness with all people (*Diary*, 491).

In her *Diary*, Faustina attempted to describe her union with God:

> My communion with the Lord is now purely spiritual. My soul is touched by God and wholly absorbs itself in Him even to the complete forgetfulness of self. Permeated by God to its very depths, it drowns in His beauty; it completely dissolves in Him — I am at a loss to describe this, because in writing I am making use of the senses; but there, in that union, the senses are not active; there is a merging of God

and the soul; and the life of God to which the soul is admitted is so great that the human tongue cannot express it (*Diary*, 767).

Union with God included union with Christ in His Passion. Saint Faustina lived St. Paul's words: "I have been crucified with Christ, and the life I live is not my own" (Gal 2:19-20). Our Lord invited her to the "exclusive privilege" of drinking from the cup that He drank (*Diary*, 1626).

He made it clear to Sister Faustina that she was participating in the great work of salvation:

I am giving you a share in the redemption of mankind (*Diary*, 310).

Help Me, My daughter, to save souls. Join your sufferings to My Passion and offer them to the heavenly Father for sinners (*Diary*, 1032).

Faustina did join her sufferings with Jesus' Passion. On Holy Thursday of 1934, after hearing Him ask her to make an offering of herself for sinners, she made an act of oblation. Later, she recorded it in her *Diary*:

Before heaven and earth, before all the choirs of Angels, before the Most Holy Virgin Mary, before all the Powers of heaven, I declare to the One Triune God that today, in union with Jesus Christ, Redeemer of souls, I make a voluntary offering of myself for the conversion of sinners, especially for those souls who have lost hope in God's mercy. This offering consists in my accepting, with total subjection to God's will, all the sufferings, fears, and terrors with which sinners are filled. In return, I give them all the consolations which my soul receives from my communion with God. In a word, I offer everything for them: Holy Masses, Holy Communions, penances, mortifications, prayers (*Diary*, 309).

Later, Faustina reflected:

From this moment on, I live in the deepest peace, because the Lord Himself is carrying me in the hollow of His hand. He, Lord of unfathomable mercy, knows that I desire Him alone in all things, always and everywhere (*Diary*, 1264).

She learned mercy and humility, and throughout her life, she found rest by total trust in the Lord's merciful Heart:

Christ and Lord, You are leading me over such precipices that, when I look at them, I am filled with fright, but at the same time I am at peace as I nestle close to Your Heart. Close to Your Heart, I fear nothing. In these dangerous moments, I act like a little child, carried in its mother's arms; when it sees something which menaces it, it clasps its mother's neck more firmly and feels secure (*Diary*, 1726).

This deep trust in Jesus enabled her to embrace His will as her own and develop the spirituality that would transform not only her life but also the lives of generations to come.

CHAPTER 3

❖❖❖❖❖

The Spiritual Life of St. Faustina

BASIC SPIRITUALITY

The basic spirituality of St. Faustina is the fundamental spirituality of all saints: union with God, built on humble obedience to His will. It is a union of love, received by total abandonment to the Lord. United perfectly with God, the saint becomes a channel for divine love to flow freely to others. His or her life becomes the fulfillment of the great commandment: Love God, and love your neighbor.

In more than three dozen *Diary* entries, Faustina writes of such union with God. She speaks of how the love of God penetrated her heart and whole being:

> At that very moment, I felt some kind of fire in my heart. I feel my senses deadening and have no idea of what is going on around me. I feel the Lord's gaze piercing me through and through. I am very much aware of His greatness and my misery. An extraordinary suffering pervades my soul, together with a joy I cannot compare to anything. I feel powerless in the embrace of God. I feel that I am in Him and that I am dissolved in Him like a drop of water in the ocean. I cannot express what takes place within me; after such interior prayer, I feel strength and power to practice the most difficult virtues. I feel dislike for all things that the world holds in esteem. With all my soul I desire silence and solitude (*Diary*, 432).

Again, she wrote:

> But when I recovered my senses, I felt the strength and courage to do God's will; nothing seemed difficult to me; and whereas I had previously been making excuses to the Lord, I now felt the Lord's courage and strength within me, and I said to the Lord, "I am ready for every beck and call of Your will!" (*Diary*, 439).

Already here on earth we can taste the happiness of those in heaven by an intimate union with God, a union that is extraordinary and often quite incomprehensible to us. One can attain this very grace through simple faithfulness of soul (*Diary*, 507).

DEVOTION TO MARY, MOTHER OF GOD

Faustina had a special devotion to Our Lady, who sometimes appeared to her and gave her counsel. From Mary, Faustina deepened her understanding of the importance of the virtues of humility, purity, and the love of God. Mary cared for Faustina as a special child, and instructed her to live always in an intimate union with God. (See more on her devotion to the Mother of God in Chapter 4: "Faustina: A Blending of East and West.")

DESIRE TO BE A SAINT

Throughout her life, Faustina desired to attain sainthood. It was a bold desire to love God as no one has ever loved Him:

My Jesus, You know that from my earliest years I have wanted to become a great saint; that is to say, I have wanted to love You with a love so great that there would be no soul who has hitherto loved You so (*Diary*, 1372).

Her resolution to be a saint was "extremely pleasing" to the Lord, and He gave her the conviction that she would attain this destiny. She wanted this sanctity in order to be useful to the Church. She understood that her actions would have a great influence on the whole Church:

I strive for the greatest perfection possible in order to be useful to the Church. Greater by far is my bond to the Church. The sanctity or the fall of each individual soul has an effect upon the whole Church (*Diary*, 1475).

Faustina embraced humility, knowing it as the acceptance of our nothingness, or "misery," as she often named it. Humility is the awareness of and response to the fact that *all is a gift*. All we are, all we have, all we do, is the gift of God. Her humble response was thanksgiving and praise for His great love and mercy.

She heard the will of God for her life through Scripture, the Church, and her superiors, and through God's word implanted in her heart. She heard and obediently acted upon it.

By canonizing Faustina, the Church officially recognized her humble obedience and her heroic practice of faith, hope, and love. Thus, Faustina's lifelong desire was realized.

THE UNIQUE FEATURES OF THE SPIRITUALITY OF ST. FAUSTINA

Though all saints share the basic spirituality of union with God, each also has unique features that distinguish him or her from others. Faustina is a special model of sanctity for our time because of her intense focus on trust in Jesus, The Divine Mercy, and the whole mystery of mercy that He revealed to her. Her life not only makes others aware of the availability of God's limitless mercy, but it also alerts us to the urgent need for that mercy in our day. Therefore, the two main features of her spirituality are trust and mercy.

TRUST

Father Ignatius Rozycki, at the request of the then Archbishop Karol Wojtyla (Blessed John Paul II), in the 1960s and 1970s studied very thoroughly the *Diary of St. Faustina* and described the central message of the *Diary* as "Trust in God's Mercy." In my translation of the Polish,

Fr. Rozycki defined *trust* as "*hope* based on *faith* and expressed in *love*."

Trust is more than faith in God. It includes hope, which is reliance upon Jesus and His promises, as well as love. Pope John Paul II developed the fuller meaning of trust in his encyclical *Mother of the Redeemer*. He reflected on the main theme of his letter using the words of St. Elizabeth: "Blest is she who trusted [believed] that the Lord's word to her would be fulfilled" (Lk 1:45). "To believe [trust]," he says, "means to 'abandon oneself to the truth of the word of the living God'" (14).

For Faustina, trust was a total abandonment and reliance upon "the truth of the word of the living God."

Examples of trust in the life of St. Faustina are found throughout her *Diary*. Our Lord taught her about the trust He wants of those seeking to be holy:

> **Let souls who are striving for perfection particularly adore My mercy, because the abundance of graces which I grant them flows from My mercy. I desire that these souls distinguish themselves by boundless trust in My mercy. I Myself will attend to the sanctification of such souls. I will provide them with everything they will need to attain sanctity. The graces of My mercy are drawn by means of one vessel only, and that is — trust. The more a soul trusts, the more it will receive** (*Diary*, 1578).

A *Diary* entry that shows her extreme trust is one made when she renewed her total gift of self to the Lord. He then told her that there was still more to give:

> Jesus said to me, **My daughter, you have not offered Me that which is really yours.** I probed deeply into myself and found that I love God with all the faculties of my soul and, unable to see what it was that I had not yet given to the Lord, I asked, "Jesus, tell me what it is, and I will give it to You at once

with a generous heart." Jesus said to me with kindness, **Daughter, give Me your misery, because it is your exclusive property.** At that moment, a ray of light illumined my soul, and I saw the whole abyss of my misery. In that same moment I nestled close to the Most Sacred Heart of Jesus with so much trust that even if I had the sins of all the damned weighing on my conscience, I would not have doubted God's mercy but, with a heart crushed to dust, I would have thrown myself into the abyss of Your mercy. I believe, O Jesus, that You would not reject me, but would absolve me through the hand of Your representative (*Diary*, 1318).

TRANSFORMED INTO TRUST

Saint Faustina described how she was transformed from her "abyss of wretchedness" to *trust* in the Lord through a deeper conversion to Him and His ways:

> Jesus, do not leave me alone in suffering. You know, Lord, how weak I am. I am an abyss of wretchedness, I am nothingness itself; so what will be so strange if You leave me alone and I fall? I am an infant, Lord, so I cannot get along by myself. However, beyond all abandonment I trust, and in spite of my own feeling I trust, and I am being completely transformed into trust — often in spite of what I feel. Do not lessen any of my sufferings, only give me strength to bear them. Do with me as You please, Lord, only give me the grace to be able to love You in every event and circumstance. Lord, do not lessen my cup of bitterness, only give me strength that I may be able to drink it all.

> O Lord, sometimes You lift me up to the brightness of visions, and then again You plunge me into the darkness of night and the abyss of my nothingness, and my soul feels as if it were alone in the wilderness.

Yet, above all things, I trust in You, Jesus, for You are unchangeable. My moods change, but You are always the same, full of mercy (*Diary*, 1489).

TRUST LEADS TO THANKSGIVING

Saint Faustina's trust in the mercy of the Lord led her to give thanks to the Father for His great gift of mercy. She gave thanks in her suffering:

Jesus, I thank You for the daily crosses, for opposition to my endeavors, for the hardships of communal life, for the misinterpretation of my intentions, for humiliations at the hands of others, for the harsh way in which we are treated, for false suspicions, for poor health and loss of strength, for self-denial, for dying to myself, for lack of recognition in everything, for the upsetting of all my plans.

Thank You, Jesus, for interior sufferings, for dryness of spirit, for terrors, fears and uncertainties, for the darkness and the deep interior night, for temptations and various ordeals, for torments too difficult to describe, especially for those which no one will understand, for the hour of death with its fierce struggle and all its bitterness (*Diary*, 343).

The joy of thanksgiving became a way of life for her:

O my Lord, while calling to mind all Your blessings, in the presence of Your Most Sacred Heart, I have felt the need to be particularly grateful for so many graces and blessings from God. I want to plunge myself in thanksgiving before the Majesty of God … and although I will outwardly carry out all my duties, my spirit will nonetheless stand continually before the Lord, and all my exercises will be imbued with the spirit of thanksgiving (*Diary*, 1369).

For more on how you can respond with greater trust, see Chapter 6: "Our Response."

DIVINE MERCY

The second unique feature of Faustina's spirituality is her intense focus on Divine Mercy. In his encyclical on Divine Mercy, *Rich in Mercy*, Pope John Paul II called mercy "the second name of love" and the greatest attribute of God toward mankind. Divine Mercy can be defined in various ways: as God's love poured out in creating, redeeming, and sanctifying us; as love poured out upon sinners; as love of the unlovable and forgiveness of the unforgivable.

Our Lord taught St. Faustina about the mystery of His mercy and His desire that her heart be a channel of His mercy to the world:

> **My daughter, know that My Heart is mercy itself. From this sea of mercy, graces flow out upon the whole world. No soul that has approached Me has ever gone away unconsoled. All misery gets buried in the depths of My mercy, and every saving and sanctifying grace flows from this fountain. My daughter, I desire that your heart be an abiding place of My mercy. I desire that this mercy flow out upon the whole world through your heart. Let no one who approaches you go away without that trust in My mercy which I so ardently desire for souls** (*Diary*, 1777).

Devotion to the merciful Heart of Jesus was central in the spirituality of St, Faustina, as well as in her mission: "O sweetest Heart of my Lord, full of pity and unfathomable mercy, I plead with You for poor sinners. O Most Sacred Heart, Fount of Mercy from which gush forth rays of inconceivable graces upon the entire human race, I beg of You light for poor sinners" (*Diary*, 72).

THE GOSPEL ELEMENTS OF HER SPIRITUAL LIFE

The basic pattern of the spiritual life of St. Faustina followed the life of Jesus, as did the lives of other mystics and saints. Indeed, we, as disciples of Christ, are all called to model out spiritual lives after the rhythm of Jesus' own. The pattern echoes the trilogy of the paschal mystery: Jesus died, rose by the Spirit, and reigns over the kingdom of God.

In the Gospels, this three-step pattern is seen in the lives of Jesus' disciples: They died to self, rose with their Savior, and with Him, reign over the kingdom. As in Faustina's life, these steps are first purgative, ridding oneself of sin and self-absorption. Next, they are illuminative, leading one to deeper spiritual understanding. Lastly, they are unitive, bringing the soul closer to oneness with God.

MYSTICS AND SAINTS

Each of the mystics and saints followed this triad approach, but in a unique way. Saint John of the Cross progressed from "*nada*," or nothingness, through "*todo*," or completeness, to union. His way is sometimes called "the dark way." Saint Ignatius of Loyola, following "the discerning way," advanced from desolation, through revelation, and arrived at consolation. The way of St. Faustina can be called "the merciful way." She moved through misery, into mercy, and finally into union with her Lord.

These three elements of spirituality — death by repentance of sin, resurrection through yielding to the Holy Spirit, and residing in the kingdom by abiding in God's love — are repeated as one grows in holiness. They are like waltz steps, and the Lord leads us in ascending spirals as we move through this dance of the Holy Spirit to the house of the Father.

THE MERCIFUL WAY

Gleaned from her *Diary*, Faustina's merciful way expresses the Gospel elements of death, resurrection, and the kingdom. Sister Faustina followed "the little way" of St. Thérèse of Lisieux, who put a special focus on littleness and on love. Faustina, who had a great devotion to St. Thérèse (see *Diary*, 150), focused particularly on one's misery and complete trust in God's mercy. She wrote:

> One day during Holy Mass, the Lord gave me a deeper knowledge of His holiness and His majesty, and at the same time I saw my own misery. This knowledge made me happy, and my soul drowned itself completely in His mercy. I felt enormously happy (*Diary*, 1801).

The Lord told Sr. Faustina to write about the merciful way for the sake of the miserable:

> **Write this for the benefit of distressed souls: when a soul sees and realizes the gravity of its sins, when the whole abyss of the misery into which it immersed itself is displayed before its eyes, let it not despair, but with trust let it throw itself into the arms of My mercy, as a child into the arms of its beloved mother. These souls have a right of priority to My compassionate Heart, they have first access to My mercy. Tell them that no soul that has called upon My mercy has been disappointed or brought to shame. I delight particularly in a soul which has placed its trust in My goodness** (*Diary*, 1541).

THE DIVINE MERCY DEVOTION AND THE PASSION OF JESUS

Sister Faustina had a special devotion to the Passion. She meditated on it and united her sufferings with those of Jesus for the salvation of souls. She prayed especially for sinners and the dying using The Divine Mercy devotions the Lord taught her. She prayed unceasingly the Chaplet of The Divine Mercy — which focuses on the power of Jesus' Passion — as she encouraged others to do. Veneration of The Divine Mercy image was another element of her spirituality. It is an image in which the healing rays of mercy stream forth from the Lord's pierced Heart.

She also would stop at the three o'clock hour, the hour of the Lord's death on the Cross, and immerse herself in the Passion of Jesus:

> **I remind you, My daughter, that as often as you hear the clock strike the third hour, immerse yourself completely in My mercy, adoring and glorifying it; invoke its omnipotence for the whole world, and particularly for poor sinners; for at that moment mercy was opened wide for every soul. In this hour you can obtain everything for yourself and for others for the asking; it was the hour of grace for the whole world —** mercy triumphed over justice (*Diary*, 1572).

For St. Faustina, the celebration of the Feast of Divine Mercy was the culmination of all the devotions to The Divine Mercy. Like the crucified Jesus, she thirsted for souls, who can receive the Lord's forgiveness and mercy in an extraordinary way on the Feast of Mercy. In all things, she sought to join her sufferings to those of her Lord for the salvation of souls:

> Jesus looked at me and said, **Souls perish in spite of My bitter Passion. I am giving them the last hope of salvation; that is, the Feast of My Mercy. If they will not adore My mercy, they will perish for all eternity** (*Diary*, 965).

> After some time, He said, **I thirst. I thirst for the salvation of souls. Help Me, My daughter, to save**

souls. Join your sufferings to My Passion and offer them to the heavenly Father for sinners (*Diary*, 1032).

Faustina summarized her spiritual life as being "drowned" in His mercy, and in her final *Diary* entry, she encapsulated her spirituality:

And, although I am such misery, I do not fear You, because I know Your mercy well. Nothing will frighten me away from You, O God, because everything is so much less than what I know [Your mercy to be] — I see that clearly (*Diary*, 1803).

Throughout her life, in her misery, she knew God's mercy and trusted in Him. She lived and died "the merciful way."

CHAPTER 4

❖❖❖❖❖

Faustina:
A Blending of
East and West

"Promoting the restoration of unity among all Christians is one of the chief concerns of the Second Sacred Ecumenical Council of the Vatican." This opening statement of the Second Vatican Council's *Decree on Ecumenism* established the commitment of the Church to Christian unity, which Pope John Paul II carried out as a major thrust of his pontificate. He elaborated on this theme in his encyclical *That They May Be One (Ut Unum Sint)*. His apostolic letter *The Eastern Light (Orientale Lumen)* is an appeal to the Christians of East and West to restore unity.

Saint Faustina fulfills the very core of this call to unity. Her life, mission, and spirituality blend elements of both Eastern and Western Church traditions. Her desire for holiness extended to Church unity, especially through her prayers and sacrifices.

'THE SPARK' FROM POLAND: WHERE EAST AND WEST MEET

Saint Faustina Kowalska writes in her *Diary*:

> As I was praying for Poland, I heard the words: **I bear a special love for Poland, and if she will be obedient to My will, I will exalt her in might and holiness. From her will come forth the spark that will prepare the world for My final coming** (*Diary*, 1732).

This mysterious spark from Poland can be seen as a combination of several people and events: St. Faustina and the message of Divine Mercy, St. Maximilian Kolbe and the role of Mary and the Holy Spirit, Blessed John Paul II's consecrating all to Mary and consecrating the world to Divine Mercy, and Lech Walesa and the Solidarity movement, which helped topple Soviet communism. These people and their works, individually and together, are sparks that continue to ignite both the East and the West.

The Polish Church is a fascinating combination of Eastern and Western spirituality, with Poland in central Europe serving as a crossroads between the East and West. Before Poland's official date of conversion in A.D. 966, the missionary apostle St. Cyril and his brother, St. Methodius, brought the Christian faith from Constantinople to Moravia, and southeastern Poland.

In *Orientale Lumen*, Pope John Paul II elaborates on the rich treasures that are integral to the Church of the East. Many of them are evident not only in Polish Catholic spirituality but also in the spirituality of The Divine Mercy as revealed to and lived out by St. Faustina. In *Orientale Lumen*, Pope John Paul II exhorts us to implore The Divine Mercy for unity of the Churches of the East and West.

As John Paul II put it on Divine Mercy Sunday in 1994, St. Faustina Kowalska is "the great apostle of Divine Mercy in our time." Her message, exemplified by her life, is the spark that will enkindle the unity of the Churches of the East and West that is to prepare for the final coming of the Lord. She lived an amazing blend of Eastern and Western spirituality. Her life helps unlock the mysteries of both.

ICONS AND OTHER DEVOTIONS

A variety of Eastern elements have become part of Polish Catholic devotional life over the centuries and were woven into the life of St. Faustina. The Eastern tradition of icons is one example. In his book *Behold the Beauty of the Lord: Praying with Icons*, Henri Nouwen says that the "Byzantine fathers focus on gazing." Icons are painted for the purpose of helping the one who gazes at them to enter into an experience of prayer. Icons may appear flat and stylized to one more accustomed to Western religious art. However, as Nouwen explains in his book, "They do not reveal themselves to us at first sight. It is only gradually, after a patient, prayerful presence that they start speaking to us. And as they speak, they speak more to our inner than to our outer senses. They speak to the heart that searches for God" (Nouwen, *Behold the Beauty of the Lord.* Notre Dame, Ind.: Ave Maria Press, 1987, p. 13).

In Poland, the appreciation of icons is seen in the veneration of the icon of Our Lady of Czestochowa and many others in parish churches and shrines throughout the country. Most homes have a prayer corner honoring the household icon. Faustina herself obtained permission to visit the icon of Our Lady of Czestochowa, where she spent hours in prayer before the image.

The blessing of food baskets at Easter and the sharing of the bread wafer (*oplatek*) at the Vigil of Christmas are other Polish customs. Sharing the wafer was a significant moment in the spiritual life of St. Faustina on Christmas Eve (see *Diary*, 435, 524, 845, 1438).

Common hymns such as the Thrice-Holy Hymn and those of St. Ephraim, the Good Friday Lamentations, the burial service of Our Lord, and the Easter Sunday Mass at dawn are other traditional practices of Polish Catholics.

THE WESTERN STYLE ICON OF JESUS, THE DIVINE MERCY

The image of Jesus, the Divine Mercy, as painted by Eugene Kazimirowski under the direction of St. Faustina is what I call a "Western Icon." Granted, that it is not "written" or painted as Eastern icons are, with inverse perspective so that the figure of Jesus draws you inward. Rather, in positive perspective, Jesus comes outward to the viewer. The image of The Divine Mercy does portray the essence of icons, namely, that of light coming out of darkness and a portrayal of the Passion, death, and Resurrection of Jesus.

The image of The Divine Mercy, I love to paint or "write," is like a "multi-exposure photo" of Holy Thursday, Good Friday, Easter Sunday, Mercy Sunday, and Pentecost —

alluding to all these events of the paschal mystery in one image of the crucified and risen Christ.

The image of The Divine Mercy, as Jesus appeared to St. Faustina, is described in superlative terms by Pope John Paul II in his last book, *Memory and Identity*. He describes it as an apt depiction of "the supreme revelation" of "Christ, crucified and risen," showing us that through His saving love, "God can always draw good from evil":

> God can always draw good from evil, He wills that all should be saved and come to knowledge of the truth (cf. 1 Tim 2:4): God is Love (cf. 4:8). Christ, crucified and risen, just as he appeared to Sister Faustina, is the supreme revelation of this truth (John Paul II, *Memory and Identity*. New York, N.Y.: Rizzoli, 2005, p. 55).

Further, the essential aspects of icons in depicting Christ and the paschal mystery are described with remarkable clarity by then Cardinal Joseph Ratzinger (now Pope Benedict XVI) in his book *The Spirit of the Liturgy*. It's almost as if he is looking at an image of The Divine Mercy as he writes:

> The images of the history of God in relation to man do not merely illustrate the succession of past events but display the inner unity of God's action In this way they have a reference to the Sacraments, above all, to Baptism and the Eucharist, and, in pointing to the Sacraments, they are contained within them. Images thus point to a presence; they are essentially connected with what happens in the liturgy. Now history becomes sacrament in Christ, who is the source of the Sacraments. Therefore, the icon of Christ is the center of sacred iconography. The center of the icon of Christ is the Paschal Mystery: Christ is presented as the crucified, the risen Lord, the One who will come again and who here and now hiddenly reigns over all. Every image of Christ must contain these three essential aspects of the mystery of

Christ and, in this sense, must be an image of Easter (Joseph Cardinal Ratzinger, *the Spirit of the Liturgy*. San Francisco, Calif.: Ignatius Press, 2000, p. 132).

Cardinal Ratzinger gives us a magnificent evaluation of The Divine Mercy image as the icon *par excellence* of the crucified and risen Christ associated with Easter!

TREASURES OF THE CHRISTIAN EAST IN THE LIFE OF ST. FAUSTINA

SACRED LITURGY AND EUCHARIST

Using the rich experiences of faith in the Eastern Churches enumerated by Pope John Paul II in *Orientale Lumen*, one is able to see how Faustina integrated treasures of the East into her spiritual life. One such treasure is devotion to the sacred liturgy, especially the Holy Eucharist. The key to the life of Sr. Maria Faustina of the Most Blessed Sacrament was the Holy Eucharist. Almost every page of her *Diary* makes a reference to it.

There are a number of "special" aspects of her relationship to the Holy Eucharist, among them her profound understanding of the mystery of this gift of God. She describes it as the greatest gift of His presence.

PARTICIPATION IN DIVINE LIFE THROUGH THE HOLY TRINITY

The goal of the Christian life, as seen from the perspective of the East, is participation in God's life through communion with the mystery of the Trinity. Saint Faustina prayed for transformation into the living image and likeness of God, being drawn into the Holy Trinity:

My Jesus, penetrate me through and through so that I might be able to reflect You in my whole life. Divinize me so that my deeds may have supernatural value (*Diary*, 1242).

She also attempts to describe her experience of divinization:

I saw the joy of the Incarnate Word, and I was immersed in the Divine Trinity. When I came to myself, longing filled my soul, and I yearned to be united with God (*Diary*, 1121).

DIVINIZATION IN THE SACRAMENTS THROUGH THE HOLY SPIRIT

The reality of divinization, or the understanding of St. Irenaeus's assertion that "God passed into man so that man might pass into God" (*Against Heresies*), is part of the heritage of the Eastern Churches. In the *Diary of St. Faustina*, we read about her desire to become transformed into a living, "sacrificial host":

Jesus, transform me, miserable and sinful as I am, into Your own self (for You can do all things), and give me to Your Eternal Father. I want to be a sacrificial host before You, but an ordinary wafer to people. I want the fragrance of my sacrifice to be known to You alone (*Diary*, 483).

The experience of being a living, sacrificial host — hidden, broken, and given — was the central experience of her life. She knew it most profoundly in conjunction with the Holy Eucharist, either during Mass and Holy Communion or during Adoration of the Blessed Sacrament.

THE VIRGIN MARY, MOTHER OF GOD AND ICON OF THE CHURCH

Mary holds a special place in the Eastern Church. Saint Faustina honored the Mother of God in a unique way. On the day of her perpetual vows, Faustina addressed Mary and prayed:

> Mother of God, Most Holy Mary, my Mother, you are my mother in a special way because your beloved Son is my Bridegroom, and thus we are both your children. For your Son's sake, you have to love me. O Mary, my dearest Mother, guide my spiritual life in such a way that it will please your Son (*Diary*, 240).

This prayer was answered in an extraordinary way when Mary appeared to her and said:

> *My daughter, at God's command I am to be, in a special and exclusive way your Mother; but I desire that you, too, in a special way be my child* (*Diary*, 1414).

On the Feast of the Annunciation, March 25, 1936, Mary appeared to Sr. Faustina explaining her mission: "*Speak to the world about* [my Son's] *great mercy and prepare for His second coming.*" Mary's role was to prepare Faustina by being a mother to her, guiding and teaching her about the life of union with God, and strengthening her in sufferings by suffering along with her (see *Diary*, 25, 309, 316, 635).

Sister Faustina prayed to the Mother of God for this mission throughout her life. She regularly celebrated the feasts of Mary with special anticipation and joy. The Holy Rosary of the Blessed Virgin Mary was part of her prayer.

Faustina reflected that "the more I imitate the Mother of God, the more deeply I get to know God" (*Diary*, 843). For Faustina, Mary was truly her mother, and she could nestle close to her Immaculate Heart like a child (see *Diary*, 1097).

THE TRINITY: UNKNOWN, DIVINE

In *Orientale Lumen*, Pope John Paul II notes the deep sense of mystery in the Eastern Churches. He reiterates their sense of God's essence being unknowable. We can only know that God *is*. From her experience, Sr. Faustina wrote many entries on the mystery of the Holy Trinity. This is one example:

> On one occasion I was reflecting on the Holy Trinity, on the essence of God. I absolutely wanted to know and fathom who God is. … In an instant my spirit was caught up into what seemed to be the next world. I saw an inaccessible light, and in this light what appeared like three sources of light which I could not understand. And out of that light came words in the form of lightning which encircled heaven and earth. Not understanding anything, I was very sad. Suddenly, from this sea of inaccessible light came our dearly beloved Savior, unutterably beautiful with His shining wounds. And from this light came a voice which said, **Who God is in His Essence, no one will fathom, neither the mind of Angels nor of man.** Jesus said to me, **Get to know God by contemplating His attributes.** A moment later, He traced the sign of the cross with His hand and vanished (*Diary*, 30).

OTHER ELEMENTS OF EASTERN SPIRITUALITY STRESSED BY JOHN PAUL II IN *ORIENTALE LUMEN*

GOSPEL, CHURCHES, AND CULTURE

When Saints Cyril and Methodius brought their faith to new places, they were careful to adopt the customs and language of those with whom they lived. Respect for cultural differences, and taking them into account when evangelizing, is another aspect of the Eastern Churches that is echoed in the life of St. Faustina.

As requested by our Lord, she wrote everything the Lord taught her about Divine Mercy. Faustina wrote simply and clearly in her native Polish. She had only two winters of schooling, and so it is amazing that her writing is so transparent and understandable. Her great love of the Lord and His Church shines through her writing. Because of Faustina's special knowledge of The Divine Mercy, the reader easily comes to understand and share in her mission of proclaiming the message of Divine Mercy. She lived and witnessed the heart of the Gospel to ordinary people.

BETWEEN MEMORY AND EXPECTATION

The rich tradition of the Church passes on the history and truths of Jesus' life to every generation of believers. Tradition gives us continuity with the past. The Eastern Churches are particularly adept at balancing a sense of connectedness to the past while being open to God's future.

Saint Faustina was deeply rooted in the tradition of the Gospel and the Church. She shared in the life of Jesus from infancy to the Cross. While she lived a life of childlike simplicity and imitation of the Child Jesus, she also repeatedly shared in His Passion.

Faustina's mission was also one of expectation. She lived it out to prepare for the coming of the Lord. Our Lady spoke to St. Faustina about the urgency of mercy:

> *I gave the Savior to the world; as for you, you have to speak to the world about His great mercy and prepare the world for the Second Coming of Him who will come, not as a merciful Savior, but as a just Judge* (*Diary*, 635).

Faustina lived in the present with her roots sunk deeply into the past. She opened herself to prepare for and receive whatever God's future would bring.

MONASTICISM, A BRIDGE BETWEEN THE EAST AND WEST

Monastic life had its beginning in the deserts of the East. There it was seen as an expression of everyone's baptismal call. Pope John Paul II named it the "very soul of the Eastern Churches" (*Orientale Lumen*). Later, monasticism was passed on to the West, where it developed a variety of expressions. Since the monastic life is lived by monks and sisters in both the East and West, it stands as a concrete expression of the unity desired by Christ.

Saint Faustina lived the monastic life to perfection. She experienced her religious vows as a means by which God united Himself to her. She expressed her attitude toward the rule of religious life with simplicity:

> I asked the Lord to grant me the grace that my nature be immune and resist the influences that sometimes try to draw me away from the spirit of our rule and from the minor regulations. These minor transgressions are like little moths, that try to destroy the spiritual life within us, and they surely will destroy it if the soul is aware of these minor transgressions and yet disregards them as small things. I can see nothing that is small in the religious life (*Diary*, 306).

Reflecting monasticism's relevance to all the faithful, Faustina described a new congregation that would be open to all the baptized as a model of the Christian life. Under the direction of the Lord, she described three levels of community, like concentric circles: The inner circle of cloistered contemplatives begging for mercy for the world; the middle circle of active contemplatives; and the outer circle of dedicated laity doing works of mercy.

BETWEEN THE WORD AND THE EUCHARIST

One facet of monasticism shared by the East and West is the ideal of living both in personal response to the Word of God and in communal celebration of the Eucharist. The latter is the culmination of prayer life, which plunges the monastic into relationship with the ecclesial community.

Saint Faustina's life was truly suspended between the two poles: the Word of God and the Eucharist. She lived the Word of God, especially the Beatitudes. Toward the end of her life, Jesus Himself directed her meditation of the Gospel according to St. John:

> **Today, My daughter, for your reading you shall take chapter nineteen of St. John's Gospel, and read it, not only with your lips, but with your heart** (*Diary*, 1765).

The culmination of her prayer life was the Eucharist.

LITURGY FOR THE WHOLE MAN, THE WHOLE COSMOS

As Pope John Paul II says in *Orientale Lumen*, the liturgy of the Eastern Churches strives to involve the entire person in its celebration. All are called, body and soul, to praise and to beauty. Along with humanity, all creation is gathered into the Eucharist of the Lord.

The Liturgy of the Eucharist was central to the life of St. Faustina. Holy Communion was a "common-union-in-Christ," a union with Christ, and all members of the Church in heaven and earth. Through this union with Christ, Faustina implored mercy on the world.

The special place of the Holy Eucharist in her life can be summed up in her official name, Sr. Maria Faustina of the Most Blessed Sacrament and in the name she called herself: "My name is to be 'sacrifice'" (*Diary*, 135). Her greatest desire was to be Eucharist: hidden like Jesus, blessed by her union with the Lord, broken like Jesus in the Passion, and totally given for the salvation of souls.

A CLEAR LOOK AT SELF-DISCOVERY

To those desiring true self-discovery, the East offers the school of contemplative gazing upon Christ, which is aided by the use of icons. The more one trains the inner eye to look in this way, the more one becomes like Christ. Every moment becomes a moment of conversion. Eventually, one is able to recognize one's own sin and let go of what keeps one from being filled with God's Spirit.

Every page of Faustina's *Diary* is a record of her intimate union with Christ. Her whole being was turned to Him in constant conversation. Aware of her misery and nothingness, she plunged into the ocean of Divine Mercy with utter trust:

> You know, Lord, how weak I am. I am an abyss of wretchedness, I am nothingness itself. ... However, beyond all abandonment I trust, and in spite of my own feeling I trust, and I am being completely transformed into trust — often in spite of what I feel (*Diary*, 1489).

With great devotion, Faustina did come to the merciful Heart of Jesus in a profound union of hearts, and she found the rest of peace. She took up His Cross as a victim of love for the sake of others. She learned mercy and humility from Jesus who formed her after the model of His own Heart.

A FATHER IN THE SPIRIT

In both Eastern and Western monasticism, individuals are often given a spiritual director. These guides share their Spirit-given gift of helping each person in their care to discern his or her path to God.

Our world desperately needs such spiritual guides. Saint Faustina was aware of the need of a spiritual guide. She pleaded with the Lord until she received a special spiritual father in the person of Fr. Michael Sopocko:

> Oh, if only I had had a spiritual director from the beginning, then I would not have wasted so many of God's graces. ... Oh, how careful confessors should be about the work of God's grace in their penitents' souls! This is a matter of great importance. By the graces given to a soul, one can recognize the degree of its intimacy with God (*Diary*, 35).

By her example and the wisdom recorded in her *Diary*, Faustina herself has become a much needed spiritual guide for our time.

COMMUNION AND SERVICE

As a monk becomes more detached from things that draw him away from God and grows in communion with the Lord, his prayer is more identified with the prayer of Christ. He shares in God's love for humanity and creation. In prayer, he invokes the Holy Spirit on the world. Such communion leads to the desire to serve others. Evangelization in its many forms is an important expression of service born of such a relationship with God.

Saint Faustina was in close communion with the Lord, and it was because of this union that her great mission of service was so powerful. In the *Diary* text selected for the Liturgy of the

Hours for her feast on October 5, she describes her mission of pleading for mercy in order that souls come to know God:

> O my God, I am conscious of my mission in the Holy Church. It is my constant endeavor to plead for mercy for the world. I unite myself closely with Jesus and stand before Him as an atoning sacrifice on behalf of the world. God will refuse me nothing when I entreat Him with the voice of His Son. My sacrifice is nothing in itself, but when I join it to the sacrifice of Jesus Christ, it becomes all-powerful and has the power to appease divine wrath (*Diary*, 482).

RELATIONSHIP WITH GOD

Union with God is a great mystery! How can a mere creature be united in an intimate way with Almighty God? It is a mystery of mercy. It is all a gift of love and can only be explained by love alone. God our Creator is in love with us. Our perfection is our union with God. Molded in the image of the Son by the Holy Spirit, the monk strives to become the "icon of the Icon."

The texts of the *Diary of St. Faustina* on union with God reveal an extraordinary call to her by Christ to an intimate spiritual union with Him. The purpose of this gift of union is to enable Faustina to do a great work and to resonate with kindred souls for guidance.

In a simple, humble way, she describes the characteristics of union with God. It is an intimate, close, and continuous presence of God that penetrates and permeates her whole being. What a "mystery of mercy" that our God should delight to dwell in the hearts of His creatures!

SILENCE: THE LANGUAGE OF GOD

The wisdom of the Eastern tradition teaches that the more one increases in knowledge of God, the more one realizes that God is unknowable. Only through what Pope John Paul II calls "adoring silence" (*Orientale Lumen*, 16) does one grow closer to experiencing God's presence. Saint Faustina learned this mysterious language of God called silence:

> The Holy Spirit does not speak to a soul that is distracted and garrulous. He speaks by His quiet inspiration to a soul that is recollected, to a soul that knows how to keep silence (*Diary*, 553).

We all need to be in silent adoration of the living God. Before His mystery of mercy, we have no words adequate to express our response. How we need the witness of St. Faustina in our time of a chaotic flood of words, words, and more words. Our hearts need to explore with a burst of adoration the mystery of God's mercy, present in our hearts. We need to live in silent spiritual communion with Love, which is poured into our hearts by the gift of the Holy Spirit.

THE TREASURES OF WESTERN CHRISTIANITY IN THE LIFE OF ST. FAUSTINA

EUCHARIST, THE BLESSED VIRGIN MARY, PETER

Saint Faustina also lived the three treasures of the West in the way that they had developed over the centuries: the Eucharist, Mary, and Peter. The Holy Eucharist is the summit of mediated graces in the Sacraments. Mary is the Queen of mediated intercession. Peter is the Vicar of Christ, the "prime minister" of mediated authority.

Mediation was a real issue of difference between Catholicism and Reformation Protestantism, which focused so strongly on the divinity of the Lord that it neglected the full appreciation of His humanity. The Catholic response was to focus on the incarnate Word, who truly became flesh and used creation to mediate His grace, intercession, and authority.

In the life of St. Faustina, we find her dedication and devotion to the Holy Eucharist expressed in both the celebration of Holy Mass and Adoration of the reserved Blessed Sacrament. When she was in her final sickness, an angel came to bring her Holy Communion. She spent every free moment in Adoration of the Blessed Sacrament.

Faustina's devotion to the Mother of God expressed itself in her recognition of her greatness by honoring her in her various titles. Faustina often made novenas in preparation for Mary's great feasts: the Immaculate Conception, the Assumption, Our Lady of Czestochowa, and Our Mother of Mercy. Above all, Faustina's devotion was to be a special daughter and imitate Mary's virtues.

Faustina's respect and obedience to authority, including her religious superiors, was exceptional. In all matters, she deferred to her confessor, spiritual director, bishop, and the Holy Father. She regularly prayed for those in authority.

CLASSIC ATONEMENT

Besides the three Catholic treasures of the Eucharist, Mary, and Peter, St. Faustina lived and proclaimed a balanced, classic atonement. She knew that Christ redeemed us by His Passion, death, and Resurrection. She also recognized that we must cooperate with His grace by our trust in Him, receive His mercy, and share it with our neighbor.

This message of a balanced and classic atonement means that we cannot merit our justification or the forgiveness of our sins, but we do merit our growth in holiness and our eternal life. (See the *Catechism of the Catholic Church*, 2006- 2011.) We draw upon the atonement of Jesus Christ for the forgiveness of our sins and those of the whole world (see 1 Jn 2:2, NIV).

Faustina is a model of holiness and of evangelization. She is a witness of a life of mercy, bringing together the various treasures of both Eastern and Western spirituality. She is a model for Church unity. She is the "spiritual guide" that we so need in our time. She herself is the message of Divine Mercy. She became the "icon of the Icon," a transforming presence of Jesus Christ, Mercy Incarnate.

CHAPTER 5

❖❖❖❖❖

Faustina:
Saint for the
Third Millennium

SPREAD OF THE DIVINE MERCY MESSAGE AND DEVOTION

Two years after the death of Faustina, the devotion to The Divine Mercy began to spread in Vilnius, which is in present-day Lithuania. Having used a booklet of prayers for this devotion assembled by Fr. Sopocko, the sisters of Faustina's own order — the Sisters of Our Lady of Mercy — did not know that she was the author. Mother Michael Moraczwaka informed them in 1941 of Sr. Faustina's mission.

Soon the message and devotion had spread across Poland. It was carried to other countries by soldiers who became acquainted with it during World War II. A Marian priest, Fr. Joseph Jarzebowski, MIC, brought the message to the United States in 1941 after a miraculous escape from war-torn Europe. Upon arriving, he persuaded his fellow Marians to spread it in the U.S. and around the world.

Then, on March 6, 1959, after studying some incomplete and inaccurate accounts of Faustina's visions and mission, the Holy See prohibited further spread of the message and devotion, pending clarification of its concerns. Most locations where the devotion had been practiced responded to the "Notification" by discontinuing the prayers and veneration of The Divine Mercy image. However, the convent of the Sisters of Our Lady of Mercy in Lagiewniki, with the permission of their archbishop, continued their devotions and their display of The Divine Mercy image. This is where St. Faustina was buried.

Tellingly, this ban on the message and devotion was prophesied by Sr. Faustina, who told her spiritual director, Fr. Michael Sopocko, that he would suffer much as a result of the prohibition:

> Once as I was talking with my spiritual director, I had an interior vision — quicker than lightning — of

his soul in great suffering, in such agony that God touches very few souls with such fire. The suffering arises from this work. There will come a time when this work, which God is demanding very much, will be as though utterly undone. And then God will act with great power, which will give evidence of its authenticity. It will be a new splendor for the Church, although it has been dormant in it from long ago. That God is infinitely merciful, none can deny. He desires everyone to know this before He comes again as Judge. He wants souls to come to know Him first as King of Mercy. When this triumph comes, we shall already have entered the new life in which there is no suffering. But before this, your soul [of the spiritual director] will be surfeited with bitterness at the sight of the destruction of your efforts (*Diary*, 378).

The ban would continue for nearly 20 years, and Fr. Sopocko would, indeed, suffer much, dying in 1975, three years before the prohibition was lifted.

ST. FAUSTINA AND POPE JOHN PAUL II

The influence of St. Faustina on Blessed John Paul II began in the early 1940s during World War II when he was in the clandestine seminary in Krakow, Poland. His classmate, who became Cardinal Andrew Deskur, told him about the mystic Sr. Faustina Kowalska and the message of Divine Mercy that she had received from the Lord. During that time, Karol Wojtyla worked as a forced laborer in the Solvay plant, which could be seen from the convent cemetery where Faustina was buried. He reportedly would visit the grave of Sister Faustina on his way home from work at the Solvay plant.

During his years in Krakow, first as a priest and then as a bishop, archbishop, and cardinal, he made use of the convent as a place of retreat and gave retreats there as well.

Then, as the faithful in Poland told Archbishop Karol Wojtyla of their desire to have Sr. Faustina raised to the honors of the altar, he decided to confer with Cardinal Alfred Ottaviani during the Second Vatican Council. Cardinal Ottaviani told him to gather the sworn testimonies of those who knew her, while they were still alive.

Archbishop Wojtyla delegated his auxiliary bishop, Julian Groblicki, to begin the Informative Process of the life and virtues of Sr. Faustina. In September 1967, the process was completed, and in January 1968, the Process of Beatification was inaugurated.

Because of the positive outcome of the Informative Process, inquiries from many places — especially from Poland, the Marians in the U.S., and in particular from Cardinal Wojtyla — were sent to the Vatican's Sacred Congregation for the Doctrine of the Faith. They asked whether the prohibitions of the 1959 "Notification" were still in effect. In response to these inquiries, the Vatican Congregation issued a new "Notification" dated April 15, 1978, which stated:

> This Sacred Congregation, having now in [its] possession the many original documents, unknown in 1959; having taken into consideration the profoundly changed circumstances, and having taken into account the opinion of many Polish Ordinaries, declares no longer binding the prohibitions contained in the quoted "Notification" [of 1959].

Six months after the Vatican lifted the ban, Cardinal Wojtyla was elected Pope John Paul II. We shall soon see how his papacy seems to have fulfilled the part of St. Faustina's prophecy about what would happen in the Church *after* the ban was lifted: "And then God will act with great power, which will give evidence of [the message and devotion's] authenticity. It will be a new splendor for the Church" (*Diary*, 378).

RICH IN MERCY, DIVES IN MISERICORDIA

Divine Mercy was clearly on the mind of John Paul II early in his papacy. On the First Sunday of Advent, November 30, 1980, he published his second encyclical letter, *Rich in Mercy* (*Dives in Misericordia*), in which he describes the mercy of God as the presence of love that is greater than evil, greater than sin, and greater than death. In it, he summons the Church to plead for God's mercy on the whole world.

The publishing of his second encyclical was, in fact, a significant event in the life of the Holy Father and in his relationship to Faustina and The Divine Mercy message and devotion. As evidence of this, in *Witness to Hope: The Biography of Pope John Paul II*, George Weigel shares from a personal interview in 1997 with John Paul II about the encyclical. It reveals Faustina's influence on him as he began to write it:

> As Archbishop of Krakow, Wojtyla had defended Sr. Faustina when her orthodoxy was being posthumously questioned in Rome, due in large part to a faulty translation into Italian of her diary, and had promoted the cause of her beatification. John Paul II, who said that he felt spiritually "very near" Sr. Faustina, had been "thinking about her for a long time" when he began *Dives in Misericordia*. (Weigel, *Witness to Hope*. New York, N.Y.: HarperCollins, 1999, p. 387.)

Further, Pope John Paul II himself wrote in striking terms in his final book about his encyclical *Rich in Mercy* (*Dives in Misericordia*) and St. Faustina's strong influence on him:

> [T]he reflections offered in *Dives in Misericordia* were the fruit of my pastoral experience in Poland, especially in Krakow. That is where Saint Faustina Kowalska is buried, she who was chosen by Christ to be a particularly enlightened interpreter of the truth of Divine Mercy. For Sister Faustina, this truth led to

an extraordinarily rich mystical life. She was a simple, uneducated person, and yet those who read the *Diary* of her revelations are astounded by the depth of her mystical experience (John Paul II, *Memory and Identity*. New York, N.Y.: Rizzoli, 2005, pp. 5-6).

There are more examples of the influence of Divine Mercy and Faustina on Pope John Paul II's life, to which he personally testified.

On November 22, 1981, Pope John Paul II made his first public visit outside of Rome — following a lengthy recuperation from medical complications he had suffered in the aftermath of the attempt on his life earlier that year on May 13. He traveled on the Feast of Christ the King to the Shrine of Merciful Love in Collevalenza, near Todi, Italy. There, within a few days, an international congress was held to reflect on the encyclical *Rich Mercy* (*Dives in Misericordia*).

After celebrating the Holy Sacrifice of the Eucharist, he made a strong public declaration about the importance of the message of mercy right from the beginning of his papacy:

A year ago I published the encyclical *Dives in Misericordia*. This circumstance made me come to the Sanctuary of Merciful Love today. By my presence I wish to reconfirm, in a way, the message of that encyclical. I wish to read it again and deliver it again.

Right from the beginning of my ministry in St. Peter's See in Rome, I considered this message my special task. Providence has assigned it to me in the present situation of man, the Church, and the world. It could be said that precisely this situation assigned that message to me as my task before God (John Paul II at The Shrine of Merciful Love in Collevalenga, Italy, November 22, 1981).

BLESSED FAUSTINA

On Mercy Sunday, April 10, 1991, two years before his beat-ification of Sr. Faustina, John Paul II spoke about Sr. Faustina, relating her to his encyclical on mercy and emphasizing her role in bringing this message of mercy to the world:

> The words of the encyclical on Divine Mercy (*Dives in Misericordia*) are particularly close to us. They recall the figure of the Servant of God, Sr. Faustina Kowalska. This simple woman religious particularly brought the Easter message of the merciful Christ closer to Poland and the whole world.

Then, on Mercy Sunday, April 18, 1993, Sr. Faustina was beatified by Pope John Paul II in St. Peter's Square. He began his homily with a quotation from her *Diary*:

> "I clearly feel that my mission does not end with death, but begins," Sr. Faustina wrote in her *Diary*. And it truly did! Her mission continues and is yielding astonishing fruit. It is truly marvelous how her devotion to the merciful Jesus is spreading in our contemporary world and gaining so many human hearts! This is doubtlessly a sign of the times — a sign of our twentieth century. The balance of this century, which is now ending, in addition to the advances which have often surpassed those of pre-ceding eras, presents a deep restlessness and fear of the future. Where, if not in the Divine Mercy, can the world find refuge and the light of hope? Believers understand that perfectly.

MERCY: HOPE FOR THE WORLD

"Where, if not in the Divine Mercy, can the world find refuge and the light of hope?" became an important theme of John Paul II's pontificate.

In his *Regina Caeli* talk of April 23, 1995, immediately after he had celebrated Divine Mercy Sunday at Holy Spirit Church in Sassia, Rome, John Paul II exhorted us to personally embrace this hope-filled message of mercy and forgiveness. He also emphasized the example of then Blessed Faustina, whom he had beatified two years earlier:

> In a special way, today is the Sunday of thanksgiving for the goodness God has shown man in the whole Easter mystery. This is why it is also called the *Sunday of Divine Mercy*. Essentially, God's mercy, as the mystical experience of Blessed Faustina Kowalska, who was raised to the honors of the altar two years ago, helps us to understand, reveals precisely this truth; good triumphs over evil, life is stronger than death and God's love is more powerful than sin. All this is manifested in Christ's Paschal Mystery, in which God appears to us as He is: a tender hearted Father, who does not give up in the face of His children's ingratitude and is always ready to forgive.

> Dear brothers and sisters, we must personally experience this mercy if, in turn, we want to be capable of mercy. *Let us learn to forgive!* The spiral of hatred and violence which stains with blood, the path of so many individuals and nations, can only be broken by the *miracle of forgiveness* (emphasis in original).

Then, when Pope John Paul II made a pilgrimage to the Shrine of The Divine Mercy in Lagiewniki, Poland, on June 7, 1997, he prayed at the tomb of Faustina. He also addressed the Sisters of Our Lady of Mercy in a very personal way, reflecting on Divine Mercy and giving an amazing personal witness to the influence of then Blessed Faustina and her message:

> I have come here to this shrine as a pilgrim to take part in the unending hymn in honor of Divine Mercy. The psalmist of the Lord had intoned it [in

Psalm 89:2], expressing what every generation preserved and will continue to preserve as a most precious fruit of faith.

There is nothing that man needs more than Divine Mercy — that love which is benevolent, which is compassionate, which raises man above his weakness to the infinite heights of the holiness of God.

In this place we become particularly aware of this. From here, in fact, went out the message of Divine Mercy that Christ Himself chose to pass on to our generation through Blessed Faustina.

And it is a *message that is clear and understandable for everyone*. Anyone can come here, look at this image of the merciful Jesus, His Heart radiating grace, and hear in the depths of his own soul what Blessed Faustina heard: **Fear nothing; I am with you always** (*Diary*, 586).

And if this person responds with a sincere heart: "*Jesus, I trust in You*," he will find comfort in all his *anxieties and fears*. ... The message of Divine Mercy has always been near and dear to me. It is as if history had inscribed it in the tragic experience of the Second World War. In those difficult years it was a *particular support and an inexhaustible source of hope*, not only for the people of Krakow but for the entire nation.

This was also my personal experience, which I took with me to the See of Peter and which in a sense forms the image of this Pontificate. ...

Dear Sisters [the Sisters of Our Lady of Mercy]! An extraordinary vocation is yours. Choosing from among you, Blessed Faustina, Christ has made your congregation the guardian of this place, and at the same time He has called you to a particular apostolate, that of His mercy. ... Do not neglect any of these dimensions of the apostolate. Fulfill it in union with the Archbishop of Krakow to whose heart is so dear the devotion to the Divine Mercy and in union with the whole ecclesial community over which he presides (emphasis in original).

THE TWOFOLD CANONIZATION OF ST. FAUSTINA

A crowning moment for Faustina and her message came in 2000, during the Great Jubilee Year of the Incarnation. On Divine Mercy Sunday, April 30, 2000, before some 250,000 pilgrims and the television cameras of the world, Pope John Paul II canonized Sr. Faustina Kowalska, "the great apostle of Divine Mercy." She was the first saint of the Great Jubilee Year, and as was the case with her beatification, Divine Mercy Sunday was chosen to mark the occasion and the location was St. Peter's Square in Rome.

In fact, at the canonization of St. Faustina, John Paul II also "canonized" The Divine Mercy message and devotion by declaring the Second Sunday of Easter as "Divine Mercy Sunday" for the universal Church. Of Divine Mercy Sunday, he said in his homily: "It is important that we accept the whole message that comes to us on this Second Sunday of Easter, which from now on throughout the Church will be called 'Divine Mercy Sunday.'"

In one of the most extraordinary homilies of his pontificate, Pope John Paul II repeated three times that Sr. Faustina is "God's gift to our time." She made the message of Divine Mercy the "bridge to the third millennium." He then said:

Sister Faustina's canonization has a particular eloquence. By this act, I intend today to pass this message on to the new millennium. I pass it on to all people, so that they will learn to know ever better the true face of God and the true face of their brethren. In fact, love of God and love of one's brothers and sisters are inseparable.

Exhorting all of us to join our voices in "singing of the mercies of the Lord forever" (Ps 89:2) with "Mary most holy, Mother of Mercy," and St. Faustina, "this new saint who sings of mercy," John Paul II ended the homily with these stirring words:

> And you, Faustina, a gift of God to our time, a gift from the land of Poland to the whole Church, obtain for us an awareness of the depth of Divine Mercy. Help us to have a living experience of it and to bear witness to it among our brothers and sisters. May your message of light and hope spread throughout the world, spurring sinners to conversion, calming rivalries and hatred, and opening individuals and nations to the practice of brotherhood. Today, fixing our gaze with you on the face of the Risen Christ, let us make our own your prayer of trusting abandonment and say with firm hope: Christ Jesus, I trust in You! *Jezu, ufam tobie!*

It's interesting that we find an echo of Pope John Paul II calling "Faustina, a gift of God to our time, a gift from the land of Poland to the whole Church" in his last book, which was published five years after the canonization. In fact, when he makes his point about Faustina's "patrimony" of Divine Mercy being of "great importance" for the whole Church and "not only for Poles," John Paul places it in the context of Faustina's beatification and canonization:

> Here I should like to return to what I said about the experience of the Church in Poland during the period of resistance to communism. It seems to me to have a universal value. I think that the same applies to Sister Faustina and her witness to the mystery of Divine Mercy. The patrimony of her spirituality was of great importance, as we know from

experience, for the resistance against the evil and inhuman systems of the time. The lesson from all this is important not only for Poles, but also in every part of the world where the Church is present. This became clear during the beatification and canonization of Sister Faustina. It was as if Christ had wanted to say through her: "Evil does not have the last word!" The Paschal Mystery confirms that good is ultimately victorious, that life conquers death and that love triumphs over hate (John Paul II, *Memory and Identity*, p. 55).

On a personal note, John Paul II was deeply moved at the canonization of his beloved Sister Faustina. "This is the happiest day of my life," the Pope reportedly told Dr. Valentin Fuster on the day of the canonization. Dr. Valentin was the cardiologist who investigated the healing of Fr. Ron Pytel, which was recognized as the miracle needed for the canonization of Faustina. The doctor was one of the principal guests at a buffet held at the Vatican after the canonization.

Finally, concerning Faustina's canonization, it's fascinating that one of her prophecies appears to have been fulfilled. The canonization was celebrated concurrently in Rome and at St. Faustina's convent chapel in Lagiewniki, Poland. At both locations, large screen televisions were set up for a simulcast — with live images shared simultaneously by those celebrating.

Many people believe that Sr. Faustina prophesied this simulcast celebration in a vision back in 1937:

I took part in [a] solemn celebration simultaneously here [in Lagiewniki] and in Rome, for the celebration was so closely connected with Rome that, even as I write, I cannot distinguish between the two, but I am writing it down as I saw it. ... The crowd was so enormous that the eye could not take it all in. ... The same celebration was held in Rome, in a beautiful church, and the Holy Father, with all the clergy, was celebrating this Feast [of Mercy] (*Diary*, 1044).

JOHN PAUL II'S ENTRUSTMENT OF THE WORLD TO DIVINE MERCY

Another mercy milestone for Faustina and her mission came on August 17, 2002, when Pope John Paul II solemnly entrusted the world to Divine Mercy at the newly constructed International Shrine of The Divine Mercy in Lagiewniki, Poland, where the great apostle of Divine Mercy lived her last years and was buried. The Pope also came to consecrate the new shrine as a basilica.

He chose to open his homily with a passage from St. Faustina's *Diary* and then immediately made reference to her and "the inconceivable and unfathomable mystery of God's mercy":

> O incomprehensible and limitless Mercy Divine,
> To extol and adore You worthily, who can?
> Supreme attribute of Almighty God,
> You are the sweet hope of sinful man (*Diary*, 951).

> Today, I repeat these simple and straightforward words of Saint Faustina, in order to join her and all of you in adoring the inconceivable and unfathomable mystery of God's mercy. Like Saint Faustina, we wish to proclaim that apart from the mercy of God there is no hope for mankind. We desire to repeat with faith: *Jesus, I trust in You!*

> This proclamation, this confession of trust in the all-powerful love of God, is especially needed in our own time, when mankind is experiencing bewilderment in the face of many manifestations of evil. *The invocation of God's mercy* needs to rise up from the depth of hearts filled with suffering, apprehension, and uncertainty, and at the same time yearning for an infallible source of hope (emphasis in the original.)

Then, before he solemnly entrusted the world to Divine Mercy, Pope John Paul II again referred to St. Faustina and a key *Diary* passage. The prophetic passage mentions "the spark" from Poland that will prepare the world for Christ's final coming. Many think that the passage, at least in part, refers to St. Faustina and The Divine Mercy message, as well as John Paul II and his ministry as the Great Mercy Pope:

> Today, therefore, in this Shrine, I will *solemnly entrust the world to Divine Mercy.* I do so with the burning desire that the message of God's merciful love, proclaimed here through Saint Faustina, *may be made known to all the peoples of the earth* and fill their hearts with hope. May this message radiate from this place to our beloved homeland and throughout the world. May the binding promise of the Lord Jesus be fulfilled: From here there must go forth "the spark which will prepare the world for His final coming" (*Diary*, 1732).
>
> This spark needs to be lighted by the grace of God. *This fire of mercy needs to be passed on to the world. In the mercy of God the world will find peace and mankind will find happiness!* I entrust this task to you, dear Brothers and Sisters, to the Church in Krakow and Poland, and to all the [devotees] of Divine Mercy who will come here from Poland and from throughout the world. *May you be witnesses to mercy!* (emphasis in original).

We will see later how John Paul II's entrustment of the world to Divine Mercy and this prophetic passage from St. Faustina's *Diary* have inspired World Apostolic Congresses on Mercy in the life of the Church.

THE DEATH OF JOHN PAUL II, HIS LAST MESSAGE OF MERCY

It was altogether fitting that Blessed John Paul II went home to God on Saturday, April 2, 2005, on the Vigil of Divine Mercy Sunday, after his trusted personal secretary, Archbishop

Stanislaus Dziwisz, celebrated the Vigil Mass for the feast in his presence.

Significantly, he received *Viaticum* — his final Holy Communion — at the Mass for his journey home. This great Pope who established Divine Mercy Sunday for the universal Church knew well of the unfathomable graces promised in the *Diary of St. Faustina* to those who receive Holy Communion worthily on the feast day. In fact, when he died at 9:37 p.m., it was already Divine Mercy Sunday in most of the Eastern part of the world.

Certainly, Mary, Our Mother of Mercy, and St. Faustina, the great Apostle of Divine Mercy, were both there to welcome him home to the Father's house.

In his final illness, Pope John Paul II had prepared a written message for Divine Mercy Sunday 2005. It became his last message for Divine Mercy Sunday, an annual practice that he had started in 1991. The message was shared posthumously with the faithful gathered in St. Peter's Square on April 3, Divine Mercy Sunday. It was like a last will and testament of Divine Mercy, with the final lines invoking the essence of The Divine Mercy message and devotion entrusted to St. Faustina. It's almost as if Faustina was peeking over his shoulder and inspiring him as he wrote it:

> As a gift to humanity, which sometimes seems bewildered and overwhelmed by the power of evil, selfishness, and fear, the Risen Lord offers His love that pardons, reconciles, and reopens hearts to love. It is a love that converts hearts and gives peace. How much the world needs to understand and accept Divine Mercy!

> Lord, [You] who reveal the Father's love by Your death and Resurrection, we believe in You and confidently repeat to You today: Jesus, I trust in You, have mercy upon us and upon the whole world. Amen (John Paul II, Divine Mercy Sunday, April 3, 2005).

In this last will and testament of mercy for John Paul II, "How much the world needs to understand and accept Divine Mercy!" is like a cry of the heart. Then, the Great Mercy Pope sums up Faustina's message of mercy with a prayer of the heart: "Jesus, I trust in You, have mercy upon us and upon the whole world. Amen." "Jesus, I trust in You" is the motto of the message that appears on every image of The Divine Mercy, while the words "have mercy upon us and upon the whole world" refer to the Chaplet of Divine Mercy.

FAUSTINA'S CONTINUING MISSION OF MERCY

POPE BENEDICT XVI'S KEY INSIGHT ON FAUSTINA AND JOHN PAUL II

As the successor to John Paul II, the Great Mercy Pope, Benedict XVI is serving as the guarantor of John Paul's legacy of mercy and St. Faustina's continuing mission of mercy. This has been particularly clear in his annual messages for the celebration of Divine Mercy Sunday and the anniversary of Blessed John Paul II's death. Benedict is our Mercy Pope, declaring on Mercy Sunday in 2006 that devotion to Divine Mercy is "an integral dimension of a Christian's faith and prayer" and then on Divine Mercy Sunday in 2008, saying, "Mercy is the central nucleus of the Gospel message."

In his statements on these and other occasions, Pope Benedict has developed a key insight into the relationship between St. Faustina and Blessed John Paul II: St. Faustina is the mystic and prophet of Divine Mercy, while John Paul II is her interpreter.

We see this in Pope Benedict's reflections at his General Audience in St. Peter's of May 31, 2006. It comes after his pastoral visit to Poland, which included a visit to the International Shrine of The Divine Mercy in Lagiewniki, Poland, where St. Faustina lived and was buried:

> It was here at the neighbouring convent that Sr. Faustina Kowalska, contemplating the shining wounds of the Risen Christ, received a message of trust for humanity which John Paul II echoed and interpreted and which really is a central message precisely for our time: Mercy as God's power, as a divine barrier against the evil of the world.

Notice how Benedict speaks of John Paul II "echo[ing] and interpret[ing]" "a message of trust for humanity" that Sr. Faustina received from the Risen Christ. Further, he describes it as "a central message precisely for our time."

Earlier, on Divine Mercy Sunday, April 23, 2006, Pope Benedict connected the mystic and her interpreter. He noted in his *Regina Caeli* message that "the Servant of God John Paul II, highlighting the spiritual experience of a humble Sister, St. Faustina Kowalska, desired that the Sunday after Easter be dedicated in a special way to Divine Mercy; and Providence disposed that he would die precisely on the eve of this day in the hands of Divine Mercy."

Perhaps, the greatest example of Pope Benedict reflecting on this special relationship came on April 2, 2008, during Holy Mass on the third anniversary of John Paul II's death. In his homily, Benedict presents St. Faustina as "a prophetic messenger of Divine Mercy" amid "the terrible tragedies of the 20th century" that Karol Wojtyla (the future Pope John Paul II) and his fellow Poles experienced, referring especially to the Nazi invasion and occupation of Poland during World War II:

> God's mercy as [Pope John Paul II] himself said, is a privileged key to the interpretation of his Pontificate. He wanted the message of God's merciful love to be made known to all and urged the faithful to witness to it (cf. Homily at Krakow-Lagiewniki, August 17,

2002). This is why he raised to the honors of the altar Sr. Faustina Kowalska, a humble Sister who, through a mysterious divine plan, became a prophetic messenger of Divine Mercy. The Servant of God John Paul II had known and personally experienced the terrible tragedies of the 20th century and for a long time wondered what could stem the tide of evil. The answer could only be found in God's love. In fact, only Divine Mercy is able to impose limitations on evil; only the almighty love of God can defeat the tyranny of the wicked and the destructive power of selfishness and hate. For this reason, during his last visit to Poland, he said on his return to the land of his birth: "Apart from the mercy of God there is no other source of hope for mankind" (Homily at Krakow-Lagiewniki, August 17, 2002).

In this homily, Pope Benedict observes that "for a long time" Karol Wojtyla had "wondered what could stem the tide of evil," based on the tragedies he witnessed in Poland. Benedict then concludes that Sr. Faustina's prophetic revelations of mercy provided the key to overcoming evil for the young Wojtyla. Thus, on his last visit to his homeland, as Pope John Paul II, he could confidently declare, "Apart from the mercy of God there is no other source of hope for mankind."

Significantly, in giving this homily, Pope Benedict inaugurated the first World Apostolic Congress on Mercy (WACOM), held in Rome on April 2-6, 2008. As we shall see, this first World Congress — which was held with Pope Benedict's support and participation — represents another milestone in Blessed John Paul's legacy of mercy and in Faustina's continuing mission of mercy.

WORLD APOSTOLIC CONGRESSES ON MERCY

First, what exactly are World Apostolic Congresses? And why are they significant in the life of the Church?

World Apostolic Congresses involve the faithful gathering from around the world in a prominent city to celebrate a particular mystery of the faith. Such congresses are significant because they have the backing of the Vatican and are celebrations of the universal Church.

International Eucharistic Congresses started in the 19th century and then World Marian Congresses at the beginning of the 20th century. Now, the first World Apostolic Congress on Mercy was held in 2008, at the beginning of the 21st century.

These Apostolic Congresses typically involve talks, prayer, time for Eucharistic Adoration, and celebration of the Sacraments to help the faithful deepen their understanding of the particular mystery of the faith and live it — whether the theme is the Holy Eucharist, the Blessed Virgin Mary, or Divine Mercy. Further, such Apostolic Congresses are held every several years. For example, the second World Apostolic Congress on Mercy is slated for October 1-5, 2011, in Krakow, ending on the feast of St. Faustina.

Now that we know a bit about Apostolic Congresses, let's talk about how they got started through the inspiration of Blessed John Paul II and his beloved Sister Faustina. It had to do with Pope John Paul II's entrustment of the world to Divine Mercy and his development on that occasion of the passage from Faustina's *Diary* about "the spark" that would come from Poland.

The initial idea of a World Mercy Congress came in July 2005 at the end of an international retreat for priests and their pastoral co-workers, which took place at the International Shrine of The Divine Mercy in Lagiewniki, Poland. The retreat was led by Cardinals Christoph Schönborn of Vienna, Austria, and Philippe Barbarin of Lyons, France, with more than 500 clergy, religious, and laity devoted to Divine Mercy in attendance.

Coming out of the retreat there in Lagiewniki, the goal for the first World Apostolic Congress was to realize Faustina and John Paul's mission of mercy when the Great Mercy Pope said right before his solemn act of entrustment: "From here there must go forth 'the spark which will prepare the world for [Jesus'] final coming' (*Diary of St. Faustina*, 1732). This spark needs to be lighted by the grace of God. This fire of mercy needs to be passed on to the world."

This goal was realized as more than 4,000 participants comprising some 200 delegations from every corner of the world convened in Rome on April 2, 2008, for the first World Apostolic Congress on Mercy. The plenary sessions were held in St. John Lateran Basilica, the cathedral of the Bishop of Rome, and prominent cardinals and bishops attended.

As for Pope Benedict, not only did he open the Congress with Holy Mass, he also addressed the delegates of the Apostolic Congress at its conclusion on April 6, 2008, in his *Regina Caeli* message. He used the forceful language of a "mandate" in encouraging the delegates to "go forth and be witnesses of God's mercy." He also emphasized God's mercy as "a source of hope for every person and for the whole world":

> Yes, dear friends, the first World Congress on Divine Mercy ended this morning … . I thank the organizers, especially the Vicariate of Rome, and to all the participants I address my cordial greeting which now becomes a mandate: go forth and be witnesses of God's mercy, a source of hope for every person and for the whole world. May the Risen Lord be with you always!

Saint Faustina and Blessed John Paul II must have been rejoicing in heaven, as they saw the "fire of mercy" being "passed on to the world" by thousands of delegates who were returning home, inspired to fulfill Pope Benedict's Divine Mercy mandate. They'll undoubtedly be rejoicing again when thousands of the faithful converge on Krakow, Poland, for the second World Apostolic Congress on Mercy in October of 2011. Saint Faustina's prophecy about what would occur to The Divine Mercy message and devotion after the lifting of the ban is being fulfilled in our time:

And then God will act with great power, which will give evidence of [the message and devotion's] authenticity. It will be a new splendor for the Church, although it has been dormant in it from long ago (*Diary*, 378).

CHAPTER 6

❖❖❖❖❖❖

Our
Response

How can we best respond to God's unfathomable mercy? In this Chapter, I will describe various dimensions of our response to The Divine Mercy message and devotion given to St. Faustina. I will consider the teaching of the Church, the condition of the world desperately in need of mercy, the demands of our Lord to us through St. Faustina, and the call to be witnesses of mercy in our day, as given by Blessed John Paul II and Pope Benedict XVI. I will also suggest ways to grow in our response by trust, prayer, and study, as well as ways to proclaim Divine Mercy.

IT'S ALL ABOUT TRUST

When fears of unknown or known origin, anxieties and confusion, and resentments all converge at once, we can easily ask ourselves this question. "What is it all about?" Then, add to it worries over family and finances. Mix in strained relations with those at work and frustration with our jobs. Finally. top it off with sickness. It is then that we scream, "Lord, what is it all about? Help! Mercy!"

It is precisely, then, that we need to try to listen to the silent voice of God deep within our hearts, pleading with us, crying out like a voice in the desert, "Trust Me!" God speaks very loudly, but His language is usually silence (see *Diary*, 888). Once our hearts are stilled, His most common words to us are: "Do not be afraid. I am with you. Trust Me." This message is often found in the Sacred Scriptures, because it is so fundamental to our human predicament. Consider this verse from the Psalms: "Trust God at all times, my people! Pour out your hearts to God our refuge!" (Ps 62:9).

Trust in the Lord is *what it is all about*. Trust is the humble and free exercise of our free will, submitting our will to the will of God. It is our faith, hope, and love put into action in responding to God's great mercy. Trust is a concrete and practical way to practice humility.

It calls us to rely on God as the giver of all good gifts and the provider of all our needs. Trust is a way to proclaim the truth that God is my Creator and Redeemer who cares for me.

The powerful prayer of the heart "Jesus, I trust in You!" is our basic response to the question: "What's it all about?" It's all about trusting in Jesus, who is the Way, the Truth and the Life. In proclaiming "Jesus, I trust in You," I proclaim Jesus as the source of all grace and light in the midst of my darkness. This proclamation helps clear the cloud of fears and anxieties within and around me. It is a battle cry that pierces the gloom, drawing our attention to the victory already won in heaven by Jesus, so that the victory may be ours on earth.

The cry of "Jesus, I trust in You" is an effective plea for the coming of the kingdom where Jesus reigns, to the glory of the Father. It is a cry of victory over the works of the Evil One. Our profession "Jesus, I trust in You" proclaims to our God that "the kingdom, the power, and the glory are Yours now and forever. Amen."

Turning to the imagery of St. Faustina, trust in the Lord opens the floodgates of God's mercy upon us. God just can't resist the humble, trusting soul, and He floods it with His love and mercy. We learn this time and again in the *Diary*.

Repeatedly, in His conversations with Sister Faustina, the Lord spoke of His merciful response to souls that trust in Him: **I desire to grant unimaginable graces, He told her, to those souls who trust in My mercy. ... Sooner would heaven and earth turn into nothingness than would My mercy not embrace a trusting soul** (*Diary* 687, 1777).

Over and over again, He stressed that He could never reject a repentant heart, never refuse an appeal to His mercy:

> **I am Mercy itself for the contrite soul. ... Souls that make an appeal to My mercy delight me. To such souls, I grant even more graces than they ask. I cannot punish even the greatest sinner if he makes an appeal to My compassion** (*Diary* 1739, 1146).

THE GIFT OF GOD'S PEACE

In His conversations with Sister Faustina, The Lord emphasized the connection between turning to His mercy and finding peace:

> **The flames of mercy are burning Me. I desire to pour them out upon human souls. Oh, what pain they cause Me when they do not want to accept them!**

> **My daughter, do whatever is within your power to spread devotion to My mercy. I will make up for what you lack. Tell aching mankind to snuggle close to My merciful Heart, and I will fill it with peace** (*Diary*, 1074).

This is the peace of the Lord that we so desperately need in our lives when we are troubled or agitated. But this peace that comes from trusting in God's mercy isn't just for us individually. No, it is also for nations and the whole world. The path to peace is not found in summit meetings, stockpiling arms, or in acquiring more material goods. The path to peace is found only in trusting in God's mercy for our lives. Our Lord makes this quite clear through His powerful words to Sister Faustina: **Mankind will not have peace until it turns with trust to My mercy** (*Diary*, 300).

So, what's it all about?

Trust!

SOME TIPS FOR GROWING IN TRUST

To grow in trust, especially when you are in difficulty, try repeating over and over again, from the heart: "Jesus, I trust in You!" Make it a cry of the heart to the Lord in your immediate need. Be mindful that Jesus is Divine Mercy Incarnate — the One who stands at the door of our hearts, waiting for us to open them even a little bit (see Rev 3:20 and *Diary*, 1486, 1507). Then, He, in his great mercy, will do the rest.

We can also be mindful that we are called to sign the image of The Divine Mercy with the words "Jesus, I trust in You!" This image of Jesus is a vessel with which we are to keep coming to Him for graces in our need (see *Diary*, 327). So, in quiet moments throughout your day, gaze upon the image of the Merciful Savior. Carry the image with you on a prayer card, which you can keep in your wallet or purse. Frame a print of the image and place it in your home and office. Look for a decal or magnet, so you can display it on the fridge or the dashboard of your car. Further, look for an image of The Divine Mercy that you can use as a screensaver on your computer.

Here's another tip: In the midst of the battle, shout the victory cheer: T.R.U.S.T.

Total
Reliance
Upon
Saving
Truth

TRUST IN JESUS AND DESIRE FOR SAINTHOOD

As we grow in trusting the Lord, the greatest desire of our heart should be the call to sainthood. Our desire is to live forever with Jesus in heaven and to do His will during our life here on earth. This is the universal call to holiness for all baptized Christians. It is the strong and clear mandate given in the *Dogmatic Constitution on the Church*, one of the main documents of the Second Vatican Council.

We have seen in Faustina's great desire to be a saint the fulfillment of this mandate. By canonizing her, the Church has established her as a model of sanctity for all of us. The central message of St. Faustina's life is her complete trust in Jesus. Her great trust enabled her to attain her goal of saint-hood. In her *Diary*, she teaches us that the desire for holiness, when combined with complete trust in God's mercy, makes sainthood accessible to all of us. All God needs is "a bit of good will" from us. Then, He will do the rest:

> O my Jesus, how very easy it is to become holy; all that is needed is a bit of good will. If Jesus sees this little bit of good will in the soul, He hurries to give Himself to the soul, and nothing can stop Him, neither shortcomings nor falls — absolutely nothing. Jesus is anxious to help that soul, and if it is faithful to this grace from God, it can very soon attain the highest holiness possible for a creature here on earth. God is very generous and does not deny His grace to anyone. Indeed He gives more than what we ask of Him (*Diary*, 291).

In another passage, Jesus tells us that even "the greatest sinners" could achieve great holiness if only they would trust in His mercy:

> **My dearest secretary, write that I want to pour out My divine life into human souls and to sanctify them, if only they were willing to accept My grace. The greatest sinners would achieve great sanctity, if only they would trust in My mercy** (*Diary*, 1784).

PERSEVERANCE

We are called to persevere in our trust in the Lord, especially when we suffer or face setbacks in life. Whether the anguish was physical or spiritual, Faustina continued to trust and embrace suffering in the spirit of Jesus. The Lord told her: **Both the sinner and the righteous person have need of My mercy. Conversion, as well as perseverance, is a grace of My mercy** (*Diary*, 1577).

Our perseverance is based on our trust in the Lord and His provision for us. After all, everything that the merciful God has arranged for us to experience at every moment is the best and holiest thing possible. Therefore, we should rejoice and give thanks, with an active abandonment to God's will, not just a passive submission. In that spirit, we then do the best we can in each and every vicissitude. As we do this, we can entrust all our concerns to the merciful Heart of Jesus and to the Immaculate Heart of Mary, Mother of Mercy.

A LIFE OF PRAYER

We nurture our relationship of trust in the Lord and our desire for holiness through a life of prayer. Faustina's entire life was given to prayer. She constantly prayed for a deeper trust in the Lord Jesus. She prayed with words and in silent contemplation, keeping herself always mindful of God's indwelling presence. Such a constant attitude of prayer is possible to attain, even in the busy world.

Of course, we all are encouraged to recite the prayers of devotion to The Divine Mercy, especially praying every day at 3 p.m., the Hour of Great Mercy, and praying the Chaplet of Divine Mercy. Our Lord particularly urged Faustina to pray the chaplet at the bedside of the dying.

Saint Faustina also encourages all of us to ask for the Holy Spirit to fill us and set our hearts on fire with the love of God. She instructs the faithful to ask in prayer for God's mercy in order to forgive and to remove any obstacles to unity. Such forgiveness leads to reconciliation, which makes possible the unity that Jesus so desires. We should ask for the Holy Spirit's help in this regard with healing any grudges or resentments with family members and friends.

Further, our prayer takes the form of praise and thanksgiving. By giving thanks always and everywhere, we acknowledge that God is God, that He knows and loves us, and cares for us in every circumstance of our lives. It's so easy in the busyness of life to take God's blessings for granted. This is why it's important to always take time to praise and thank God whenever we pray. As we do, let's remember that all of God's blessings are a sign of His mercy toward us, since they are all gifts from Him.

First and foremost, St. Faustina's prayer life was grounded in reverent and frequent reception of the Sacraments, especially attendance at daily Mass, going to confession regularly, and spending time adoring Jesus present in the Blessed Sacrament. As much as our circumstances and responsibilities permit, we should seek to do likewise as the foundation of our prayer life. The Holy Eucharist and the Sacrament of Reconciliation are the great Sacraments of Mercy, bringing us the Lord's healing presence, superabundant graces, and forgiveness.

HOW DO WE SHOW MERCY?

We have been focusing on how we can receive God's mercy through trusting in Jesus and cultivating a life of prayer. Now, we shift gears to focus on how we are called to show mercy to others.

First, it's important to stress that this call to show mercy is at heart of the Gospel. We hear the beatitude of mercy in Jesus' Sermon on the Mount: "Blessed are the merciful, for they will be shown mercy" (Mt 5:7). Then, in St. Luke's Gospel, the Lord tells us, "Be merciful as your Father in heaven is merciful" (Lk 6:36 RSV). As Christians, we are called to be merciful to others in the same way God the Father is merciful to us. In a word, we are to love our neighbor in need as God has loved us.

Our Lord explained to Sister Faustina that faith alone would not suffice. **But there must also be acts of mercy**, He told her. **Even the strongest faith is of no avail without works** (*Diary*, 742).

Jesus gave her three ways to practice mercy toward our neighbor:

I am giving you three ways of exercising mercy toward your neighbor: the first — by deed, the second — by word, the third — by prayer. In these three degrees is contained the fullness of mercy, and it is an unquestionable proof of love for Me. By this means a soul glorifies and pays reverence to My mercy (*Diary*, 742).

These, then, must become our fundamental way of expressing trust in the mercy of God, By deeds of mercy, we show others how to be merciful; by our words of encouragement and advice, in preaching, teaching, and writing, we let others know of God's mercy; by prayer, we implore mercy for sinners and glorify the mercy of the Lord.

The Church has taught the works of mercy in two groups: the Corporal and Spiritual Works of Mercy. The Corporal Works of Mercy are: feeding the hungry, giving drink to the thirsty, clothing the naked, sheltering the homeless, comforting the prisoners, visiting the sick, and burying the dead. The Spiritual Works of Mercy include: teaching the ignorant, praying for the living and the dead, correcting sinners, counseling those in doubt, consoling the sorrowful, bearing wrongs patiently, and forgiving wrongs willingly.

For those who feel that these works are too dramatic, too removed from the situations we "ordinary" people encounter in our daily lives, Blessed Mother Teresa of Calcutta offers an explanation that suggests the countless opportunities we all have to be channels of His mercy. She is summing up the words of Jesus Himself in the Gospel account of the Last Judgment (see Mt 25:31-46):

Jesus says, "Whatever you do to the least of your brothers is done in my name. When you receive a little child you receive me. If in my name you give a glass of water, you give it to me." And to make sure that we understand what he is talking about, he says that at the hour of death we are going to be judged only that way. "I was hungry, you gave me to eat. I was naked, you clothed me. I was homeless, you took me in." Hunger is not only for bread; hunger is for love. Nakedness is not only for a piece of clothing; nakedness is lack of human dignity, and also that beautiful virtue of purity, and lack of respect for each other. Homelessness is not only being without a home made of bricks; homelessness is also being rejected, unwanted, unloved (*Jesus, the Word to be Spoken* Servant Books, Ann Arbor, Mich.: Servant Books/St. Anthony Messenger Press, 1998, p. 154).

Jesus emphasized to Sister Faustina that all our works of mercy are to an **unquestionable proof of our love for** [Him], and they are to become a consistent pattern in our lives. **You are to show mercy to your neighbor always and everywhere,** He explained. **You must not shrink from this or try to excuse or absolve yourself from it** (*Diary*, 742).

This would be an impossible command were it not for our spiritual foundation of trusting in Jesus, The Divine Mercy, which we covered earlier. The Lord says. **When a soul approaches Me with trust, I fill it with such an abundance of graces that it cannot contain them within itself, but radiates them to other souls** (*Diary*, 1074).

LIVING THE LORD'S PRAYER: A CALL TO LIVE MERCIFULLY

Once, when Jesus was praying in a certain place (see Lk 11:1), the sight of what He was doing fascinated His disciples, "Lord, teach us to pray," one of the them blurted out. And so, Jesus taught them, but He did more than give them words to say; He gave them a way to live, the way He Himself lived — as Mercy Incarnate.

Jesus lived for His Father, pleasing Him, doing His will to reveal Him as the Father, who is "rich in mercy" (Eph 2:4). In revealing God as the Father, He was proclaiming and establishing the kingdom of God, and in this way, He hallowed the name of the Father and did His will. He trusted in the Father to provide all His needs each day, and He forgave all who hurt Him. By His redemption on the Cross, He forgave us our sins (see Col 1:14), and by His daily living of trust and mercy, He destroyed the power of the Evil One. In a word, he lived and revealed *Mercy.*

And so for us, too, The Lord's Prayer is a way to live. We can look at this prayer and see two pivotal points: the Father and the *kingdom.* Our whole life is to be for the Father, who is "rich in mercy." His kingdom is established as we follow Him and do His will. Prayer teaches us how to do His will — by totally trusting in Him for our daily bread, which includes all our daily needs, and then by being merciful as He is merciful, forgiving others' sins as we are forgiven ours. This way, we are not put to the test, but are delivered from the prince of this world, the Evil One.

We are merciful by being continuously forgiving — 70 times seven times a day! This means forgiving in all the great and "little" things of our daily lives, forgiving ourselves, friends, family, co-workers, and even God for situations that displease us. Every time we feel ourselves getting impatient, angry, or frustrated, we have an opportunity to forgive — an opportunity to cry, "I repent, I forgive." I repent for my part in this situation, and I forgive them for their part —"Jesus, mercy!"

A beautiful example of being merciful by forgiving comes out in an incident between two women at a bookshop. The owner came into the bookshop one day, and started directing the work of the manager, and this with her usual gusto. The manager started to fume inside while trying to keep her cool on the outside. Afterwards, she went to her parish priest and vented her feelings about the interference in her work. After she had vented her anger for a while, Father interrupted with the question, "Was the owner right or wrong?"

"She was wrong!" retorted the woman with no uncertainty in her voice.

"Wonderful," Father responded, "now you are in the

perfect situation to be a Christian and forgive her!"

To be merciful is to forgive without considering the rightness or the wrongness of the situation. This is the way Christ has forgiven us, and the way we are to forgive one another.

OUR RESPONSE TO THE CHALLENGES OF ST. FAUSTINA, BLESSED JOHN PAUL II, AND POPE BENEDICT XVI

We called to be Apostles of Divine Mercy and witnesses of mercy, following the example of St. Faustina, Blessed John Paul II, and Pope Benedict XVI. Remember in particular Pope Benedict's Divine Mercy "mandate," which calls us to "go forth and be witnesses of God's mercy, a source of hope for every person and for the whole world."

How can we do this? We can start by living the ABC's of Mercy:

A: Ask for His Mercy
B: Be Merciful
C: Completely Trust in Jesus.

It is a simple summary of The Divine Mercy message and devotion. Try it! It works well as a reminder.

But there is more that is needed: study, prayer, the witness of our very lives, a relationship with Mary, and offering our sufferings and miseries for others:

STUDY: I suggest you start with helpful books of explanation: *The Divine Mercy Message and Devotion* (M17) and *Now is the Time For Mercy* (NTM). Then, learn even more about Faustina's life by reading the longer biography, *The Life of Faustina Kowalska*, by Sr. Sophia Michalenko, CMGT (DML6). Only then would I recommend reading the *Diary of St. Faustina* and daily devotionals based on the *Diary*, such as *Mercy Minutes: Daily Gems of St. Faustina to Transform Your Prayer Life* (MMIN2) and *Mercy Minutes with Jesus: Praying Daily on Jesus' Words from the Diary of St. Faustina* (MMWJ). Then, to study in more depth themes in the *Diary*, use the *Thematic Concordance to the Diary of St. Maria Faustina Kowalska* (SGD2). Also, to study Divine Mercy in the papacies of John Paul II and Benedict XVI, read *John Paul II: The Great Mercy Pope* (GMP2) and *Pope Benedict's Divine Mercy Mandate* (PBBK).

PRAYER: Frequent the Sacraments as much as possible. Take a daily prayer time and include Adoration of the Blessed Sacrament if possible. Pray the Chaplet of Divine Mercy daily and offer frequently Divine Mercy prayers that are short — especially the prayer "Jesus, I trust in You!" (For more, see the earlier section on prayer and the selection of prayers provided in Chapter 7.)

WITNESS OF OUR VERY LIVES: Tell your personal witness of mercy when asked. My advice on how to reach your parish priest with the message is to offer your help in whatever way he may suggest. Let your humble service of mercy be a living witness to him. Also, consider Faustina's advice. She instructs us to evangelize by living lives of mercy toward others. Her vision of a new congregation included a wider circle of members that could include everyone in the world. No vows would be required of this group. Acts of mercy by words, prayers, and deeds would be their duties:

A member of this group ought to perform at least one act of mercy a day; at least one, but there can be many more, for such deeds can easily be carried out by anyone, even the very poorest. For there are three ways of performing an act of mercy; the merciful word, by forgiving and by comforting; secondly, if you can offer no word, then pray — that too is mercy; and thirdly, deeds of mercy. And when the Last Day comes, we shall be judged from this, and on this basis we shall receive the eternal verdict (*Diary*, 1158).

MARY, MOTHER OF MERCY: Ask your spiritual mother to teach and guide you as she did St. Faustina. A daily renewal of your consecration to Mary is the foundation of your relationship and prayer to her. Make Faustina's consecration to Mary your own:

To The Mother of God

O Mary, my mother and my Lady, I offer you my soul, my body, my life and my death, and all that will follow it. I place everything in your hands. O my Mother, cover my soul with your virginal mantle and grant me the grace of purity of heart, soul and body. Defend me with your power against all enemies, and especially against those who hide their malice behind the mask of virtue. ... Fortify my soul that pain may not break it. Mother of grace, teach me to live by [the power of] God (*Diary*, 79, 315).

O Mary ... a terrible sword has pierced your holy soul. Except for God, no one knows of your suffering. Your soul does not break; it is brave, because it is with Jesus. Sweet Mother, unite my soul to Jesus, because it is only then that I will be able to endure all trials and tribulations, and only in union with Jesus will my sacrifices be pleasing to God. Sweetest Mother, continue to teach me about the interior life. May the sword of suffering never break me. O pure Virgin, pour courage into my heart and guard it (*Diary*, 915).

Let me offer a personal aside on devotion to Mary that shows how special we are to her as her dearly beloved children. On one of my pilgrimages to Ostra Brahma in Vilnius, Lithuania, the words Mary spoke to St. Faustina came alive to me. As Our Lady called Faustina her "special" daughter, so I heard in my heart, Mary telling me, "You are my special son":

> The Feast of the Immaculate Conception. Before Holy Communion I saw the Blessed Mother inconceivably beautiful. Smiling at me she said to me, *My daughter, at God's command I am to be, in a special and exclusive way your Mother; but I desire that you, too, in a special way, be my child* (*Diary*, 1414).

OFFERING OUR SUFFERINGS AND MISERIES

Finally, in response to God's mercy in our lives, we can offer our sufferings and miseries to the Lord for the salvation of souls. This is a beautiful and powerful act of mercy, and we all have some form of sufferings and miseries to offer the Lord.

The teaching of Sacred Scripture, the Church, and the saints tell us the purpose and value of suffering:

> **SAINT PAUL** in the Epistle to the Romans writes: "The Spirit Itself bears witness with our spirit that we are children of God, and if children, then heirs, heirs of God and joint heirs with Christ, *if only we suffer with Him* so that we may also be glorified with Him" (Rom 8:16-17) (emphasis added).

> **SAINT FAUSTINA** repeatedly in her *Diary* tells us of the great value of suffering with Christ: "Oh, if only the suffering soul knew how it is loved by God, it would die of joy and of excess happiness! Some day, we will know the value of suffering, but then we will no longer be able to suffer. The present moment is ours (*Diary*, 963). And in another passage, she

wrote: "During Holy Mass, I saw the Lord Jesus nailed upon the cross amidst great torments. A soft moan issued from His Heart. After some time, He said, **I thirst, I thirst for the salvation of souls. Help Me, My daughter, to save souls. Join your sufferings to My Passion and offer them to the heavenly Father for sinners** (*Diary*, 1032).

POPE JOHN PAUL II in *Salvifici Doloris*, his apostolic letter on the meaning of suffering, tells us, in summary, that we can offer our sufferings with the little love we do have to Jesus and His love. In doing so, we join Jesus in saving souls. Our sufferings joined to those of Jesus can bring salvation to souls! What a precious gift of mercy.

So do not waste your sufferings! What a great way to be apostles of Divine Mercy: Save souls by giving your sufferings to Jesus!

In conclusion, trust in Jesus more every day. Desire to be a saint. Frequent the Sacraments. Develop a strong prayer life. Perform works of mercy. Seek to live mercifully. Study. Pray even more. Witness to mercy. Consecrate your life to Mary. And keep offering your sufferings and miseries to the Lord.

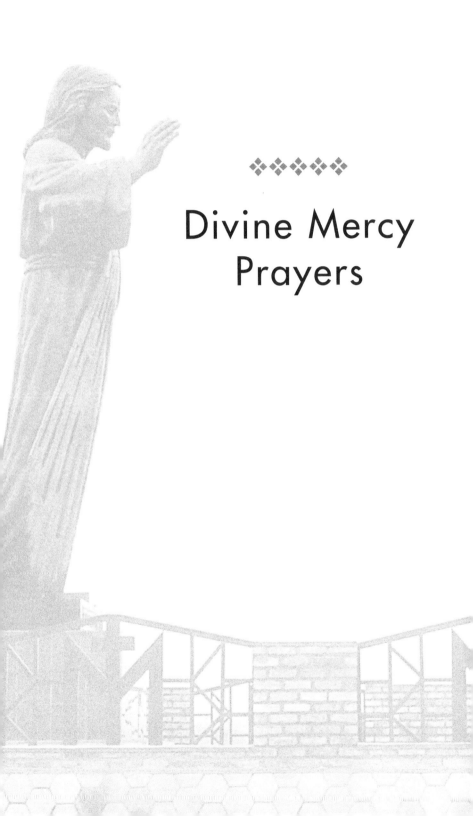

Divine Mercy Prayers

St. Faustina records a number of prayers of Divine Mercy. Three of them were taught to her by Jesus, and many others she composed and recorded in her *Diary*. The following is a selection.

These taught by our Lord to St. Faustina have a priority of honor:

1. **"Jesus, I Trust in You!"** (*Diary*, 47). *It is the shortest Divine Mercy prayer that has spread around the world, and it appears on every image of The Divine Mercy. Trust in Jesus is the summary of the message of Divine Mercy.*

2. **"O Blood and Water which gushed forth from the Heart of Jesus as a Fount of Mercy for us, I trust in You."** *Saint Faustina daily repeated this prayer as a renewal of her self-oblation* (*Diary*, 309). *She also used this prayer for the conversion of sinners* (see *Diary* 186, for the Lord's explanation).

FOR THE CONVERSION OF SINNERS

Jesus said to St. Faustina:

You always console Me when you pray for sinners. The prayer most pleasing to Me is the prayer for the conversion of sinners. Know, My daughter, that this prayer is always heard and answered (*Diary*, 1397).

On another occasion, He told her:

I desire that you know more profoundly the love that burns in My Heart for souls, and you will understand this when you meditate upon My Passion. Call upon My mercy on behalf of sinners; I desire their salvation. When you say this prayer with a contrite heart and with faith on behalf of some sinner, I will give him the grace of conversion. This is the prayer:

"O Blood and Water, which gushed forth from the Heart of Jesus as a fountain of mercy for us, I trust in You" (*Diary* 186, 187).

This promise of our Lord was specifically made to St. Faustina, but if we pray this prayer with the same purity of intention, we have reason to believe God will honor it.

3. **The Chaplet of Divine Mercy** *is highly recommended by our Lord. I would encourage you to pray it daily. It is like offering a "mini-Mass"!*

You will recite it for nine days, on the beads of the rosary, in the following manner: First of all, you will say one OUR FATHER and HAIL MARY and the I BELIEVE IN GOD. Then on the OUR FATHER beads you will say the following words: "Eternal Father, I offer You the Body and Blood, Soul and Divinity of Your dearly beloved Son, Our Lord Jesus Christ, in atonement for our sins and those of the whole world." On the HAIL MARY beads you will say the following words: "For the sake of His sorrowful Passion have mercy on us and on the whole world." In conclusion, three times you will recite these words: "Holy God, Holy Mighty One, Holy Immortal One, have mercy on us and on the whole world" (*Diary*, 476).

The following prayers composed by St. Faustina have been meaningful to me:

A PRAYER TO BE MERCIFUL, *I use this prayer daily as part of my personal devotions:*

O Most Holy Trinity! As many times as I breathe, as many times as my heart beats, as many times as my blood pulsates through my body, so many thousand times do I want to glorify Your mercy.

I want to be completely transformed into Your mercy and to be Your living reflection, O Lord. May the greatest of all divine attributes, that of Your unfathomable mercy, pass through my heart and soul to my neighbor.

Help me, O Lord, that my eyes may be merciful, so that I may never suspect or judge from appearances, but look for what is beautiful in my neighbors' souls and come to their rescue.

Help me, that my ears may be merciful, so that I may give heed to my neighbors' needs and not be indifferent to their pains and moanings.

Help me, O Lord, that my tongue may be merciful, so that I should never speak negatively of my neighbor, but have a word of comfort and forgiveness for all.

Help me, O Lord, that my hands may be merciful and filled with good deeds, so that I may do only good to my neighbors and take upon myself the more difficult and toilsome tasks.

Help me, that my feet may be merciful, so that I may hurry to assist my neighbor, overcoming my own fatigue and weariness. My true rest is in the service of my neighbor.

Help me, O Lord, that my heart may be merciful so that I myself may feel all the sufferings of my neighbor. I will refuse my heart to no one. I will be sincere even with those who, I know, will abuse my kindness. And I will lock myself up in the most merciful Heart of Jesus. I will bear my own suffering in silence. May Your mercy, O Lord, rest upon me.

You Yourself command me to exercise the three degrees of mercy. The first: the act of mercy, of whatever kind. The second: the word of mercy — if I cannot carry out a work of mercy, I will assist by my words. The third: prayer — if I cannot show mercy by deeds or words, I can always do so by prayer. My prayer reaches out even there where I cannot reach out physically.

O my Jesus, transform me into Yourself, for You can do all things (*Diary*, 163)

A PRAYER FOR MERCY ON THE WHOLE WORLD,

This prayer is used daily at the National Shrine of The Divine Mercy, Stockbridge, Massachusetts.

O greatly merciful God, Infinite Goodness, today all mankind calls out from the abyss of its misery to Your mercy — to Your compassion, O God; and it is with its mighty voice of misery that it cries out. Gracious God, do not reject the prayer of this earth's exiles! O Lord, Goodness beyond our understanding, who are acquainted with our misery through and through, and know that by our own power we cannot ascend to You, we implore You; anticipate us with Your grace and keep on increasing Your mercy in us, that we may faithfully do Your holy will all through our life and at death's hour. Let the omnipotence of Your mercy shield us from the darts of our salvation's enemies, that we may with confidence, as Your children, await Your final coming — that day known to You alone. And we expect to obtain everything promised us by Jesus in spite of all our wretchedness. For Jesus is our Hope: Through His merciful Heart, as through an open gate, we pass through to heaven (*Diary*, 1570).

If you like litanies, here is a "Litany of Trust and Praise" by St. Faustina:

SAINT FAUSTINA'S LITANY OF PRAISES TO THE DIVINE MERCY

The Love of God is the flower — Mercy, the fruit.

Let the doubting soul read these considerations on Divine Mercy and become trusting.

Divine Mercy, gushing forth from the bosom of the Father, I Trust in You.

Divine Mercy, Greatest attribute of God, I Trust in You.

Divine Mercy, incomprehensible mystery, I Trust in You.

Divine Mercy, fountain gushing forth from the mystery of the Most Blessed Trinity, I Trust in You.

Divine Mercy, unfathomed by any intellect, human or angelic, I Trust in You.

Divine Mercy, from which wells forth all life and happiness, I Trust in You.

Divine Mercy, better than the heavens, I Trust in You.

Divine Mercy, source of miracles and wonders, I Trust in You.

Divine Mercy, encompassing the whole universe, I Trust in You.

Divine Mercy, descending to earth in the Person of the Incarnate Word, I Trust in You.

Divine Mercy, which flowed out from the open wound of the Heart of Jesus, I Trust in You.

Divine Mercy, enclosed in the Heart of Jesus for us, and especially for sinners, I Trust in You.

Divine Mercy, unfathomed in the institution of the Sacred Host, I Trust in You.

Divine Mercy, in the founding of Holy Church, I Trust in You.

Divine Mercy, in the Sacrament of Holy Baptism, I Trust in You.

Divine Mercy, in our justification through Jesus Christ, I Trust in You.

Divine Mercy, accompanying us through our whole life,
    I Trust in You.
Divine Mercy, embracing us especially at the hour of death,
    I Trust in You.
Divine Mercy, endowing us with immortal life,
    I Trust in You.
Divine Mercy, accompanying us every moment of our life,
    I Trust in You.
Divine Mercy, shielding us from the fire of hell,
    I Trust in You.
Divine Mercy, in the conversion of hardened sinners,
    I Trust in You.
Divine Mercy, astonishment for Angels, incomprehensible
    to Saints, I Trust in You.
Divine Mercy, unfathomed in all the mysteries of God,
    I Trust in You.
Divine Mercy, lifting us out of every misery, I Trust in You.
Divine Mercy, source of our happiness and joy,
    I Trust in You.
Divine Mercy, in calling us forth from nothingness to
    existence, I Trust in You.
Divine Mercy, embracing all the works of His hands,
    I Trust in You.
Divine Mercy, crown of all of God's handiwork,
    I Trust in You.
Divine Mercy, in which we are all immersed, I Trust in You.
Divine Mercy, sweet relief for anguished hearts, I Trust in You.
Divine Mercy, only hope of despairing souls, I Trust in You.
Divine Mercy, repose of hearts, peace amidst fear,
    I Trust in You.
Divine Mercy, delight and ecstasy of holy souls,
    I Trust in You.
Divine Mercy, inspiring hope against all hope,
    I Trust in You.

Eternal God, in whom mercy is endless and the
treasury of compassion inexhaustible, look kindly

upon us and increase Your mercy in us, that in difficult moments we might not despair nor become
despondent, but with great confidence submit
ourselves to Your holy will, which is Love and Mercy
itself (*Diary*, 949-50).

FOR PRIESTS

O my Jesus, I beg You on behalf of the whole Church:
Grant it love and the light of Your Spirit and give
power to the words of priests so that hardened hearts
might be brought to repentance and return to You, O
Lord. Lord, give us holy priests; You Yourself maintain
them in holiness. O Divine and Great High Priest, may
the power of Your mercy accompany them everywhere
and protect them from the devil's traps and snares
which are continually being set for the souls of priests.
May the power of Your mercy, O Lord, shatter and
bring to naught all that might tarnish the sanctity of
priests, for You can do all things (*Diary*, 1052). I ask
You for a special blessing and for light, O Jesus, for the
priests before whom I will make my confessions
throughout my lifetime (*Diary*, 240).

PRAYER IN TIME OF SUFFERING — *I especially turn to this prayer when I am suffering.*

A thought of Sister Faustina:

Oh, if only the suffering soul knew how much God
loves it, it would die of joy and excess of happiness!
Some day, we will know the value of suffering, but
then we will no longer be able to suffer. The present
moment is ours (*Diary*, 693).

Jesus, do not leave me alone in suffering. You know,
Lord, how weak I am. I am an abyss of wretchedness, I
am nothingness itself; so what will be so strange if You

leave me alone and I fall? I am an infant, Lord so I cannot get along by myself. However, beyond all abandonment I trust, and in spite of my own feeling I trust, and I am being completely transformed into trust — often in spite of what I feel. Do not lessen any of my sufferings, only give me strength to bear them. Do with me as You please, Lord, only give me the grace to be able to love You in every event and circumstance. Lord, do not lessen my cup of bitterness, only give me strength that I may be able to drink it all (*Diary*, 1489).

AT THE FEET OF THE EUCHARIST

This Eucharistic prayer of combined Diary passages is a gem of St. Faustina. Her full name, chosen by lot, was the phrase added to her name: Sister Maria Faustina of the Most Blessed Sacrament:

O Jesus, Divine Prisoner of Love, when I consider Your love and how You emptied Yourself for me, my senses fail me. You hide Your inconceivable majesty and lower Yourself to miserable me. O King of Glory, though You hide Your beauty, yet the eye of my soul rends the veil. I see the angelic choirs giving You honor without cease, and all the heavenly Powers praising You without cease, and without cease they are saying: Holy, Holy, Holy.

Oh, who will comprehend Your love and Your unfathomable mercy toward us! O Prisoner of Love, I lock up my poor heart in this tabernacle that it may adore You without cease night and day. I know of no obstacle in this adoration, and even though I be physically distant, my heart is always with You. Nothing can put a stop to my love for You. No obstacles exist for me (*Diary*, 80).

O Holy Trinity, One and Indivisible God, may You be blessed for this great gift and testament of mercy (*Diary*, 81).

I adore You, Lord and Creator, hidden in the Blessed Sacrament. I adore You for all the works of Your hands, that reveal to me so much wisdom, goodness and mercy, O Lord. You have spread so much beauty over the earth, and it tells me about Your beauty, even though these beautiful things are but a faint reflection of You, Incomprehensible Beauty. And although You have hidden Yourself and concealed Your beauty, my eye, enlightened by faith, reaches You, and my soul recognizes its Creator, its Highest good; and my heart is completely immersed in prayer of adoration (*Diary*, 1692).

My Lord and Creator, Your goodness encourages me to converse with You. Your mercy abolishes the chasm which separates the Creator from the creature. To converse with You, O Lord, is the delight of my heart. In You I find everything that my heart could desire. Here Your light illumines my mind, enabling it to know You more and more deeply. Here streams of graces flow down upon my heart. Here my soul draws eternal life. O my Lord and Creator, You alone, beyond all these gifts, give Your own self to me and unite Yourself intimately with Your miserable creature (*Diary*, 1692).

O Christ, I am most delighted when I see that You are loved, and that Your praise and glory resound, especially the praise of Your Mercy. O Christ, to the last moment of my life, I will not stop glorifying Your goodness and mercy. With every drop of my blood, with every beat of my heart, I glorify Your mercy. I long to be entirely transformed into a hymn of Your glory. When I find myself on my deathbed, may the last beat of my heart be a loving hymn in praise of Your unfathomable mercy (*Diary*, 1708).

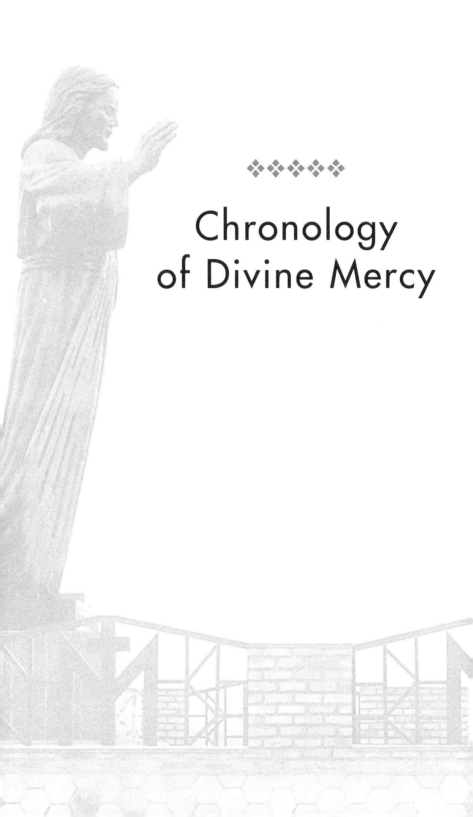

❖❖❖❖❖

Chronology
of Divine Mercy

CHRONOLOGY OF EVENTS

The main events of the life of St. Faustina Kowalska, her cause of beatification and canonization, and her ongoing mission of mercy in our time:

AUGUST 25, 1905: Sister Faustina is born Helen Kowalska in the village of Glogowiec, near Lodz, Poland.

1912: At the age of seven, Helen hears for the first time a voice in her soul, calling her to a more perfect way of life.

JUNE 19-25, 1925: At the age of 20, during the Octave of Corpus Christi, Helen makes a vow of perpetual chastity.

AUGUST 1, 1925: Helen is accepted into the Congregation of the Sisters of Our Lady of Mercy as a lay sister. She begins her postulancy at Warsaw and then leaves for Krakow to complete it.

APRIL 30, 1926: Helen begins her two-year novitiate in Krakow, receiving her religious habit and the name Maria Faustina.

FEBRUARY 22, 1931: Sister Faustina sees the Lord Jesus dressed in a white robe. Red and pale rays stream forth from the area of His Heart. **Paint an image, He tells her, according to the pattern you see, bearing the signature, "Jesus, I trust in You."**

JANUARY 2, 1934: Sister Faustina meets with the artist Eugene Kazimirowski, who, through Fr. Michael Sopocko (her spiritual director and confessor), has been commissioned to paint the image of The Divine Mercy.

JUNE 1934: The Kazimirowski painting is completed. Sister Faustina is disappointed with it and cries to the Lord, "Who will paint You as beautiful as You are?" In reply, she hears the words,

Not in the beauty of the color nor of the brush lies the greatness of this image, but in My grace (*Diary*, 313). The painting is hung in the corridor of the Bernardine Sisters' Convent near St. Michael's Church in Vilnius, where Fr. Sopocko is rector.

JULY 1934: Following the instructions of her spiritual director (Fr. Sopocko), Sr. Faustina begins keeping a personal diary, which she entitles *Divine Mercy in My Soul.*

AUGUST 1934: Sister Faustina suffers a violent attack of asthma for the first time, perhaps already due to tuberculosis, which is to cause her almost constant suffering for the few remaining years of her life.

OCTOBER 26, 1934: Sister Faustina sees the Lord Jesus above the chapel in Vilnius, with the same red and pale rays coming from the area of His Heart. The rays envelop the chapel and the students' infirmary, and then spread out over the whole world.

APRIL 26-28, 1935: During the celebration concluding the Jubilee Year of the Redemption of the world, the Kazimirowski image of The Divine Mercy is transferred to Ostra Brama (Shrine of Our Lady of Mercy in Vilnius) and placed in a high window so it may be seen from far away. This event coincides with the Second Sunday of Easter, which, according to Sister Faustina, is to be celebrated as the Feast of Divine Mercy. Father Sopocko delivers a homily about The Divine Mercy.

JANUARY 8, 1936: Sister Faustina visits Bishop Romuald Jalbrzykowski and tells him that Jesus has asked for a new congregation to be founded.

OCTOBER 5, 1936: Father Sopocko writes to Sr. Faustina, asking for the texts of the Chaplet and the Novena to The Divine Mercy.

DECEMBER 9, 1936: With her health deteriorating, Sr. Faustina is sent to the hospital in Pradnik, a sanatorium in Krakow for tuberculosis patients. Except for a few days during the Christmas season, she remains there until March 27, 1937.

DECEMBER 13, 1936: Under the appearance of her confessor, Jesus Himself hears Sr. Faustina's confession.

APRIL 4, 1937: Father Sopocko publishes an article on The Divine Mercy in the *Vilnius Catholic Weekly.*

APRIL 4, 1937: By permission of Archbishop Romuald Jalbrzykowski, the Kazmirowski image is blessed and placed in St. Michael's Church in Vilnius.

SEPTEMBER 27, 1937: Sister Faustina and Mother Irene meet with the printer who is to print holy cards bearing the image of The Divine Mercy.

NOVEMBER 1937: Through the efforts of Fr. Sopocko, the Litany, Chaplet, and Novena to The Divine Mercy are published by the J. Cebulski Press in Krakow in a pamphlet entitled "Christ, King of Mercy." On the cover of the pamphlet is a color picture representing the merciful Christ with the signature, "Jesus, I trust in You." Holy cards, bearing a copy of Kazimirowski's image of The Divine Mercy on the front, and the chaplet on the back, are also printed by Cebulski.

NOVEMBER 10, 1937: Sister Faustina and Mother Superior Irene look over the pamphlet containing the Litany, Chaplet, and Novena, to The Divine Mercy, and the Lord tells Sr. Faustina that many souls have already been drawn to Him through the image.

APRIL 21, 1938: Suffering greatly from tuberculosis, Sr. Faustina leaves the convent for her final, five-month stay at the sanatorium in Pradnik.

APRIL 22-MAY 6, 1938: For 14 days, at the sanatorium in Pradnik, Sr. Faustina receives Holy Communion from an angel.

JUNE 24, 1938: Sister Faustina sees the Sacred Heart of Jesus in the sky in the midst of a great brilliance. Rays are streaming from the wound in His side and spreading out over the entire world.

JUNE 1938: She stops writing the *Diary* due to illness.

SEPTEMBER 2, 1938: Father Sopocko visits her at the sanatorium in Pradnik and discovers her in ecstasy.

SEPTEMBER 26, 1938: Father Sopocko visits her in Krakow for the last time and notes that "she looked like an unearthly being, ... I no longer had the slightest doubt that what she had written in her *Diary* about receiving Holy Communion from an angel was really true."

OCTOBER 5, 1938: At 10:45 p.m., Sr.. Faustina dies of multiple tuberculosis in Krakow, at the age of 33.

OCTOBER 7, 1938: Her funeral coincides with the First Friday of the month and the Feast of Our Lady of the Rosary.

SEPTEMBER 1, 1939: German tanks and planes cross the Polish frontier, and the Nazis take control of Poland. In the course of the war, the city of Warsaw, along with many other Polish cities and towns, is destroyed by incendiary and demolition bombs, an apparent fulfillment of Sr. Faustina's earlier prophecy:

> One day Jesus told me that He would cause a chastisement to fall upon the most beautiful city in our country [probably, Warsaw]. This chastisement would be that with which God had punished Sodom and Gomorrah (*Diary*, 39).

SPRING, 1940: Father Joseph Jarzebowski, MIC, a Marian priest from Warsaw who had been blacklisted by the Nazi SS, hears about the devotion to The Divine Mercy at a camp in Vikomir, Lithuania.

JULY-SEPTEMBER 1940: Father Jarzebowski prays to The Divine Mercy to help him escape to America.

FEBRUARY 25, 1941: Hearing of Fr. Jarzebowski's plan to escape, Fr. Sopocko gives him a Latin memorandum outlining the message and devotion to The Divine Mercy. Father

Jarzebowski promises to do his best to keep the memorandum safe and have it printed when he reaches America. Entrusting himself and his mission to The Divine Mercy, he vows to spend the rest of his life spreading the mercy message and devotion if he reaches safety.

FEBRUARY 26, 1941: Carrying a picture of the merciful Jesus next to his heart and Fr. Sopocko's Divine Mercy memorandum in his traveling bag, Fr. Jarzebowski leaves his hiding place in Vilnius and boards an ordinary trans-Siberian train. Traveling across the whole of Russia and Siberia, he reaches Vladivostock, where the customs officer searches everything except the bag containing the memorandum. No one seems to notice that his American visa is obsolete and invalid, and he is granted Japanese transit.

When he reaches Japan, he finds $30.00 and a ticket to the United States waiting for him, sent by Fr. Joseph Luniewski, MIC, of the Marians in America. The Polish embassy validates his American visa, and he leaves for the United States.

MAY 1941: Father Jarzebowski lands on American soil. Full of gratitude to the mercy of God and remembering his promises to Fr. Sopocko, he begins to share the message and devotion of mercy privately. At a Detroit print shop, the first sample copies of the image are made.

JUNE 1941: Asked to assist as confessor at the annual retreat for the Felician Sisters in Enfield, Connecticut, Fr. Jarzebowski speaks to the sisters about the revelations to Sr. Faustina and the essence of the message and devotion to The Divine Mercy, mentioning the special graces given to him. The sisters make a copy of his brief account, and the provincial superior donates a sum of money to have several hundred copies of the image printed.

1941: At a "house meeting" in Washington, D.C., a tiny group of Marians decides to undertake as an apostolate the spreading of the message and devotion to The Divine Mercy, and they begin printing the first novena leaflets.

NOVEMBER 28, 1958: Sister Faustina's prophecy about the apparent destruction of the devotion to The Divine Mercy (see *Diary*, 378 and 1659) begins its fulfillment by a decree of condemnation due to incorrect translations in the Italian version of her *Diary*. The severe ban is mitigated by Pope John XXIII on March 6, 1959, to a "Notification" that prohibited "the spreading of the devotion according to Sr. Faustina."

OCTOBER 21, 1965: In the Archdiocese of Krakow, 27 years after the death of Faustina, Bishop Julian Groblicki, specially delegated by Archbishop Karol Wojtyla, begins the Informative Process relating to the life and virtues of Sr. Faustina. From this moment, Sr. Faustina is worthy of the title "Servant of God."

NOVEMBER 25, 1966: While the Informative Process relating to the virtues, writings, and devotion of the Servant of God Sr. Faustina is being conducted (October 21, 1965, to September 20, 1967), her remains are exhumed and translated to a tomb specially prepared for this purpose in the chapel of the Sisters of Our Lady of Mercy in Lagiewniki. Over the tomb is a black slab with a cross in the center. The slab usually has fresh flowers brought by the faithful, who plead for numerous graces through her intercession.

JUNE 26, 1967: Archbishop Karol Wojtyla becomes Cardinal Karol Wojtyla.

SEPTEMBER 20, 1967: The Archbishop of Krakow, Cardinal Karol Wojtyla, officially closes the first informative stage in the process for the beatification of the Servant of God Sr. Faustina Kowalska.

JANUARY 31, 1968: By a decree of the Sacred Congregation for the Causes of Saints, the Process of Beatification of the Servant of God Sr. Faustina Kowalska is formally inaugurated.

APRIL 15, 1978: In response to inquiries from Poland, and in particular Cardinal Wojtyla, about the "Notification" of 1959, the Sacred Congregation for the Canonization of Saints declares the Notification is no longer binding due to the changed circumstances and the opinion of many Polish ordinaries.

OCTOBER 16, 1978: Cardinal Karol Wojtyla is elected Pope John Paul II.

NOVEMBER 30, 1980: Pope John Paul II publishes his encyclical letter *Rich in Mercy* (*Dives in Misericordia*), in which he stresses that Jesus Christ has revealed God, who is "rich in mercy," as the Father. He speaks of mercy as "the most stupendous attribute of the Creator and Redeemer" (RIM, 13).

JUNE 19, 1981: The Sacred Congregation for the Causes of Saints, having completed the investigation of all available writings of the Servant of God Sr. Faustina, issues a decree stating that "nothing stands in the way of proceeding further" with her cause.

OCTOBER 8, 1981: The Sacred Congregation for the Sacraments and Divine Worship issues a decree confirming the Latin text of a Votive Mass of The Divine Mercy for the Metropolitan Archdiocese of Krakow, Poland.

APRIL 10, 1991: Pope John Paul II, at his general audience, speaks about Sr. Faustina, showing his great respect for her, relating her to his encyclical *Rich in Mercy*, and emphasizing her role in bringing the message of mercy to the world.

MARCH 7, 1992: In the presence of the Holy Father, the Congregation for the Causes of Saints promulgates the Decree of Heroic Virtues, by which the Church acknowledges that Sr. Faustina practiced all the Christian virtues to a heroic degree. As a result, she receives the title "Venerable" Servant of God, and the way is opened for verification of the miracle attributed to her intercession.

In that same year, the healing of Maureen Digan at the tomb of Sr. Faustina is recognized as a miracle by three separate panels appointed by the Sacred Congregation: first a panel of doctors, then of theologians, and finally, of cardinals and bishops.

DECEMBER 21, 1992: The Holy Father publishes the Church's acceptance of the miracle as granted through the intercession of Sr. Faustina and announces the date for her solemn beatification.

APRIL 18, 1993: St. Faustina is beatified in Rome on the Second Sunday of Easter (which our Lord has revealed to her as the "Feast of Divine Mercy").

SEPTEMBER 4, 1993: John Paul II prays the Rosary at the Shrine of Our Lady of Mercy, Ostra Brama, in Vilnius, Lithuania, where the image of the Merciful Jesus was first displayed.

SEPTEMBER 5, 1993: John Paul II kneels and prays before the image of The Divine Mercy, painted under the direction of Sr. Faustina, in the Church of the Holy Spirit, Vilnius.

JANUARY 23, 1995: Pope John Paul II grants to the Polish Bishops that the Sunday after Easter be the Sunday of Divine Mercy because of the need and desire of the faithful.

APRIL 23, 1995: Pope John Paul II celebrates Divine Mercy Sunday in Holy Spirit Church, the Shrine of The Divine Mercy in Rome (*L'Osservatore Romano*, English Edition, April 26, 1995). In his homily, he challenges us to "trust in the Lord and be apostles of Divine Mercy."

In his "*Regina Caeli*" address, he speaks of this Sunday as the day of thanksgiving for God's mercy, called the Sunday of Divine Mercy. He challenges us to personally experience this mercy in order to be merciful and forgive — and so "break the spiral of violence by the *miracle of forgiveness*" (emphasis in original).

JUNE 7, 1997: Pope John Paul II makes a pilgrimage to the Shrine of The Divine Mercy in Lagiewniki (Krakow), Poland, at the convent where the relics of Sr. Faustina are honored. He says, "The message of Divine Mercy has always been near and dear to me." John Paul II then goes on to highlight how Divine Mercy helped him and his compatriots in Poland endure "the tragic experience of the Second World War," emphasizing, "This was also my personal experience, which I took with me to the See of Peter and which in a sense forms the image of this Pontificate."

NOVEMBER 20, 1999: Pope John Paul II accepts the healing of the heart of Fr. Ronald Pytel of Baltimore, Maryland, as the miracle for the canonization of then Blessed Faustina.

APRIL 30, 2000: Pope John Paul II canonizes Sr. Faustina Kowalska and proclaims Divine Mercy Sunday for the universal Church. The canonization occurs on Divine Mercy Sunday and is held in St. Peter's Square in Rome. In his homily, he repeats three times that Sr. Faustina is "God's gift to our time." He also passes on the message of Divine Mercy to the new millennium. Of Divine Mercy Sunday, he says in his homily, "It is important that we accept the whole message that comes to us on this Second Sunday of Easter, which from now on throughout the Church will be called 'Divine Mercy Sunday.'"

APRIL 17, 2002: Pope John Paul II consecrates the Basilica of The Divine Mercy in Krakow-Lagiewniki, Poland, and entrusts the World to Divine Mercy. Before he solemnly entrusts the world to Divine Mercy, Pope John Paul says, "I do so with the burning desire that the message of God's merciful love, proclaimed here through St. Faustina, *may be made known to all the peoples of the earth* and fill their hearts with hope" (emphasis in original).

APRIL 2, 2005: Pope John Paul II dies on the Vigil of Divine Mercy Sunday. It is altogether fitting that the Great Mercy Pope who established Divine Mercy Sunday for the universal Church goes home to God on its vigil. He leaves his last annual Divine Mercy Sunday message, which is shared with the faithful in St. Peter's Square on April 3, Divine Mercy Sunday. He closes his message with this summary of The Divine Mercy message and devotion: "Jesus, I trust in You, have mercy upon us and upon the whole world. Amen."

APRIL 19, 2005: Cardinal Joseph Ratzinger is elected Pope and chooses the name of Benedict XVI. In his first message as Pope on April 20, Benedict XVI expresses "deep gratitude for a gift of Divine Mercy." He says that he considers it "a special grace" obtained for him by his predecessor, Blessed John Paul II. He goes on to say of John Paul, "I seem to feel his strong hand clasping mine; I seem to see his smiling eyes and hear his words, at this moment addressed specifically to me, 'Do not be afraid!'"

MAY 2006: Pope Benedict XVI goes on pilgrimage to Poland, the homeland of John Paul II. On his pilgrimage, Pope Benedict visits the International Shrine of The Divine Mercy in Lagiewniki, Poland. He says in his general audience of May 31 of his visit there:

> It was here in the neighboring convent that Sr. Faustina Kowalska, contemplating the shining wounds of the Risen Christ, received a message of trust for humanity which John Paul II echoed and interpreted and which really is a central message precisely for our time: Mercy as God's power, as a barrier against the evil of the world.

APRIL 2-6, 2008: The first World Apostolic Congress on Mercy is held in the Vatican. More than 4,000 participants comprising some 200 delegations from every corner of the globe convene in Rome on April 2 for the first World Apostolic Congress on Mercy. Pope Benedict XVI inaugurates the Congress by celebrating Holy Mass in St. Peter's Square on April 2, the third anniversary of the death of Blessed John Paul II. In his homily, Pope Benedict underscores John Paul II's legacy of mercy and St. Faustina as "a prophetic messenger of Divine Mercy" for John Paul in helping him make sense of the "terrible tragedies of the 20th century." The plenary sessions for the Congress are held in St. John Lateran Basilica, the cathedral of the Bishop of Rome, and many prominent cardinals and bishops attend the sessions. Then, at the conclusion of the Congress, on April 6, Pope Benedict gives his Divine Mercy mandate in his *Regina Caeli* message:

> Yes, dear friends, the first World Congress on Divine Mercy ended this morning. ... I thank the organizers, especially the Vicariate of Rome, and to all the participants I address my cordial greeting which now becomes a mandate: *go forth and be witnesses of God's mercy*, a source of hope for every person and for the whole world. May the Risen Lord be with you always! (emphasis added).

SEPTEMBER 28, 2008: The spiritual director and confessor of St. Faustina, Fr. Michael Sopocko is beatified in Bialystok, Poland, with an estimated 70,000 people attending. They include 100 religious sisters from 13 countries representing the Congregation of the Sisters of the Merciful Jesus, an order founded by Blessed Michael. Pope Benedict XVI addresses the assembly live by satellite feed from Castel Gandolfo, Italy, and says of Blessed Michael:

> At his suggestion, [Sister] Faustina described her mystical experiences and apparitions of the merciful Jesus in her well-known *Diary*. Thanks to his efforts, the image with the words, "Jesus, I trust in You" was painted and transmitted to the world. The Servant of God became known as a zealous priest, teacher, and promoter of the Divine Mercy devotion. ... My beloved Predecessor, the Servant of God John Paul II most certainly rejoices in this beatification in the Father's house.

MAY 1, 2011: The Great Mercy Pope, the Venerable Servant of God John Paul II — who died on the Vigil of Divine Mercy Sunday in 2005 — is beatified in St. Peter's Square on Divine Mercy Sunday by his successor, Pope Benedict XVI. An overflow crowd, estimated at more than 1.5 million people, attends the beatification in Rome in 2011, which comes in record-breaking time, only six years after John Paul's death in 2005. In fact, it is the largest crowd Rome has seen since John Paul's funeral. Further, it is significant that Blessed John Paul II entitled the Second Sunday of Easter as Divine Mercy Sunday when he canonized St. Faustina in 2000, which Pope Benedict highlights at the beatification. Pope Benedict says in his homily for the occasion:

> Six years ago we gathered in this Square to celebrate the funeral of Pope John Paul II. Our grief at his loss was deep, but even greater was our sense of an immense grace which embraced Rome and the whole world: a grace which was in some way the fruit of my beloved predecessor's entire life, and especially of his witness in suffering. Even then we perceived the fragrance of his sanctity, and in any number of ways God's People showed their veneration for him. For this reason, with all due respect for the Church's canonical norms, I wanted his cause of beatification to move forward with reasonable haste. And now the longed-for day has come; it came quickly because this is what was pleasing to the Lord: John Paul is blessed! ...

> Today is the Second Sunday of Easter, which Blessed John Paul II entitled Divine Mercy Sunday. The date was chosen for today's celebration because, in God's providence, my predecessor died on the vigil of this feast.

MARIAN PRESS

STOCKBRIDGE, MA

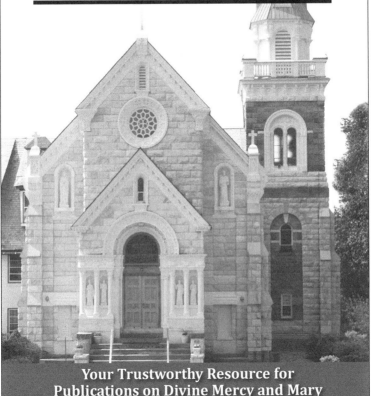

**Your Trustworthy Resource for
Publications on Divine Mercy and Mary**

PROMOTING DIVINE MERCY SINCE 1941

Marian Press, the publishing apostolate of the Marian Fathers of the Immaculate Conception of the B.V.M., has published and distributed millions of religious books, magazines, and pamphlets that teach, encourage, and edify Catholics around the world. Our publications promote and support the ministry and spirituality of the Marians worldwide. Loyal to the Holy Father and to the teachings of the Catholic Church, the Marians fulfill their special mission by:

- Fostering devotion to Mary, the Immaculate Conception.

- Promoting The Divine Mercy message and devotion.

- Offering assistance to the dying and the deceased, especially the victims of war and disease.

- Promoting Christian knowledge, administering parishes and shrines, and conducting missions.

Based in Stockbridge, Mass., Marian Press is known as the publisher of the *Diary of Saint Maria Faustina Kowalska*, and the Marians are the leading authorities on The Divine Mercy message and devotion.

Stockbridge is also the home of the National Shrine of The Divine Mercy, the Association of Marian Helpers, and a destination for thousands of pilgrims each year.

Globally, the Marians' ministries also include missions in developing countries where the spiritual and material needs are enormous.

To learn more about the Marians, their spirituality, publications, or ministries, visit **marian.org** or **thedivinemercy.org**, the Marians' website that is devoted exclusively to Divine Mercy.

Below is a view of the National Shrine of The Divine Mercy and its Residence in Stockbridge, Mass. The Shrine, which was built in the 1950s, was declared a National Shrine by the National Conference of Catholic Bishops on March 20, 1996.

© MARIE ROMAGNANO

MARIAN PRESS
STOCKBRIDGE   MA 01263

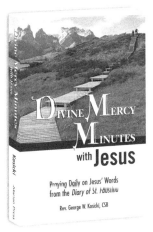

ESSENTIAL DIVINE MERCY RESOURCES

AUDIO DIARY OF SAINT MARIA FAUSTINA

You'll feel like you are actually listening to St. Faustina speak in a gentle Polish accent as she writes in her *Diary*. Hear this dramatic portrayal of the voices of Jesus and Our Lady. Gain deeper insight into Faustina's mission to share the message of Divine Mercy with the world. Includes all passages from the printed *Diary*, prayerful music, and three renditions of the Chaplet of The Divine Mercy. 33 hours on 27 CDs.

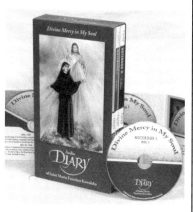

ADCD 9781596142299

DIARY OF SAINT MARIA FAUSTINA KOWALSKA: DIVINE MERCY IN MY SOUL, DELUXE LEATHER-BOUND EDITION

Share the gift of mercy with this deluxe edition of the book that has sparked The Divine Mercy movement among Christians. Pages come with gilded edges and a ribbon marker. 7 1/8" x 4 3/8", 772 pages, 37 photos.

BURGUNDY: DDBURG **9781596141896**
NAVY BLUE: DDBLUE **9781596141902**

Hardcover, Trade Paper, and Compact Editions available in English and Spanish.

ESSENTIAL DIVINE MERCY RESOURCES

The Divine Mercy

Jesus, I Trust In You!

Message and Devotion

M17 9780944203583

THE DIVINE MERCY MESSAGE AND DEVOTION

Fr. Seraphim Michalenko, MIC with Vinny Flynn and Robert A. Stackpole.

Outlining The Divine Mercy message and devotion in an easy-to-follow format, this booklet provides an overview to one of the Catholic Church's fastest growing movements. Includes all elements and essential prayers of The Divine Mercy message and devotion.

DISCOVER THE MANDATE

Pope Benedict's Divine Mercy Mandate is brilliantly written. David Came traces the thread of Divine Mercy throughout the papacy of Benedict XVI and pulls back the veil on a papal program for what it means to "go forth and be witnesses of God's mercy." This is a must-read.

— Drew Mariani, Nationally syndicated radio talk show host, author, and award-winning journalist

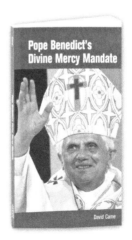

Pope Benedict's Divine Mercy Mandate

David Came

PBBK   9781596142039

ESSENTIAL DIVINE MERCY RESOURCES

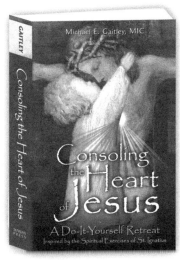

CHJ 9781596142220

CONSOLING THE HEART OF JESUS
A DO-IT-YOURSELF RETREAT

Written by
Michael E. Gaitley, MIC

Don't have time for a 30-day retreat but want to become a saint? Perfect! This book was written for you. Endorsed by EWTN hosts Fr. Mitch Pacwa, SJ, and Fr. Benedict Groeschel, CFR, this do-it-yourself retreat combines the *Spiritual Exercises of St. Ignatius* with the teachings of Saints Thérèse of Lisieux, Faustina Kowalska, and Louis de Montfort. The author, Father Michael Gaitley, MIC, has a remarkable gift for inspiring little souls to trust in Jesus, The Divine Mercy.

To make the retreat, all you need is a desire to grow in holiness and the time it takes to prayerfully read the text. Read it rapidly over a weekend or stretch it out over a couple of weeks. As you do, be prepared for a deeper, invigorating experience of the Lord's love and mercy.

428 pages. Includes bonus material in appendices.

Father
Michael Gaitley, MIC

– The voice of Christ in these pages is one that even this hopelessly distracted wife and mother of eight could hear and respond to. Reading it has been an enormous blessing to me, one that I treasure and will return to often.

— DANIELLE BEAN
Editorial Director of *Faith & Family*
magazine (FaithandFamilyLive.com)

MERCY VIEWING

GEND 9781596141759

GENERATIONS UNITE IN PRAYER: THE DIVINE MERCY CHAPLET IN SONG

This award-winning DVD recreates the beloved contemporary melody of The Divine Mercy Chaplet in Song, made popular on EWTN. Hear the voices of hundreds of children, teens, parents, and grandparents as they pray for the poor, for the dying, and the unborn. Crossing all denominational lines and spanning all generations, Christians unite to tell the world about God's mercy.

TELL ALL SOULS ABOUT MY MERCY

This DVD brings the heart of the *Diary of St. Faustina* to life! Hear the basics of these important revelations, dive deep into conversation with Jesus as He speaks with suffering souls, and join the Blessed Mother on the road to Calvary. Discover the correlation between the Shroud of Turin and the image of The Divine Mercy painted under the direction of St. Faustina by Christ's command.

TASDVD 9781596141803

CGDVD 9781596141810

CENACLE OF THE DIVINE MERCY — EWTN PROGRAM, SERIES I

Set of 4 DVDs: Join Fr. Joe Roesch, MIC, Dr. Bryan Thatcher, and Cenacle members from around the country in discussing the transformation that Divine Mercy has brought to their lives. Free companion guide included.

Companion Guide: Dive deeper into God's mercy! Each chapter expands one of the 13 topics covered in the popular EWTN television series. A must-have for each member of your prayer group.

BLESSED JOHN PAUL II
THE GREAT MERCY POPE
THE BEATIFICATION EDITION

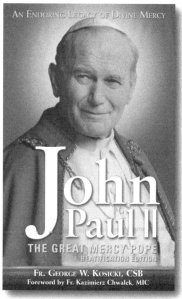

Make Blessed John Paul II's enduring legacy of Divine Mercy your own.

This book is a genuine treasure for theologians as well as the faithful who wish to make Blessed John Paul II's legacy of Divine Mercy their own.

GMP3 9781596142411

JOHN PAUL II: THE GREAT MERCY POPE
AN ENDURING LEGACY OF DIVINE MERCY

Written by Rev. George W. Kosicki, CSB
Foreword by Fr. Kazimierz Chwalek, MIC

In this masterwork that draws from all of John Paul II's writings, addresses, and homilies on Divine Mercy, Fr. George Kosicki helps us better understand that as we accept God's mercy and then go forth as witnesses to it, we are carrying on John Paul II's legacy as our own. Along with a foreword by Fr. Kazimierz Chwalek, who attended the beatification, this edition includes new chapters on the beatification and the approved miracle, a full-color photo section, and the text of Pope Benedict's homily at the beatification.